Fun on Flatwater

An Introduction to
Adirondack Canoeing

Fun on Flatwater

An Introduction to Adirondack Canoeing

Barbara McMartin

Illustrations by Gregory Palestri

Maps by W. Alec Reid

North Country Books
Utica, New York

FUN ON FLATWATER

First Printing 1995
Second Printing 1999
Revised Edition 2003

ISBN 0-925168-40-8

Library of Congress Cataloging-in-Publication Data

GV776.N72A3456 1995
797.1'22'097475—dc20
95-15935
CIP

NORTH COUNTRY BOOKS, INC.
311 Turner Street
Utica, New York 13501

For the next generation of canoeists,

the grandchildren,

Ali, Casey, Lisa, and Dan

With thanks to Betsy Folwell for editing this book and to all the friends who have canoed with us: Chuck and Edith Bennett, Lee and Georgie Brenning, Jim and Caroline Dawson, Clyde and Sally Griffen, and Stanford Pulrang. Thanks also to Brian McDonnell for advice on canoeing instructions and to Ed Ketchledge for pond information.

Working on this book has been a family affair; my son James and my daughters, Nancy and Margaret, and their husbands, Dick Loomis and Bob Lawrence, all were involved. Above all, I really appreciate the time my husband, W. Alec Reid, spent creating the computerized maps. And I am very pleased with Greg Palestri's line drawings, which add so much to the book.

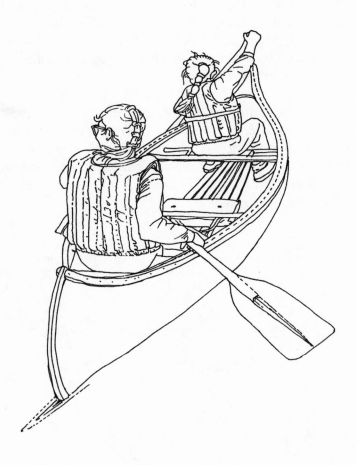

Contents

Getting Started, 9

Canoe Rentals, Outfitters, and Instruction, 29

Easy Lakes and Ponds, 30
    Adirondack Map--Campgrounds, Lakes, and Ponds, 31

Campgrounds, 32

Ponds and Lakes, 37

Streams with One Put-in, 55
Adirondack Map--Streams with One Put-in, 56
1. Auger Flats, 58
2. West Lake to Canada Lake, 59
3. East Canada Creek, 59
4. West Branch Sacandaga River, 60
5. Above Bog River Falls, 62
6. Miami River from Lewey Lake, 62
7. Black River above Kayuta Lake, 63
8. Main Branch Moose River to Nelson Lake, 64
9. Middle Branch Moose River, 64
10. South Inlet, Raquette Lake, 65
11. North Branch Saranac River, 65
12. Schroon River just below Schroon Lake, 66
13. Ausable Marsh, 67
14. Mouth of the Boquet River, 68

Longer Trips with One Put-in, 69
Adirondack Map--Longer Trips with One Put-in, 70
1. Canada Lake Outlet to Stewarts Dam, 71
2. Fall Stream, 72
3. Moffit Beach, Sacandaga Lake, to Mud Pond, 73
4. Kunjamuk River, 74
5. Cedar River Flow, 75
6. Big Moose Lake to the Eastern Inlets, 77
7. Forked Lake and Brandreth Lake Outlet, 78
8. Lake Lila, 79
9. Bog River to Hitchins Pond, 80

10. Little River, 81
11. Massawepie Mire on the Grass River, 82
12. Raquette River, 84
13. Raquette River, Axton to High Falls, 86
14. Chubb River, 87
15. Osgood River, 89
16. Rainbow and Kushaqua Lakes, 90
17. South Bay of Lake Champlain, 91

Two-Car or Shuttle Routes, 92
Adirondack Map--Shuttle Routes, 93
1. Hudson River Feeder Canal, 94
2. Black River Feeder Canal, 96
3. Hudson River, Warrensburg to Luzerne, 100
4. West Branch Sacandaga River to Shaker Place, 102
5. Black Creek, 104
6. North Branch Moose River, 106
7. Raquette Lake to Blue Mountain Lake, 108
8. Grass River, 110
9. Jones, Osgood, and Church Ponds, 112
10. Hatch Brook to Salmon River, 114
11. Hoel Pond to Long Pond, St. Regis Canoe Area, 116

More Adventures, 117
1. Whitney Park and Little Tupper Lake, 118
2. Saranac River, 120
3. The Main Branch of the Moose River, 122
4. Four-Pond Circuit in the Saranac Wild Forest, 124
Other Brochures and Canoe Possibilities, 125

Index to Terms and Waters Described, 118

Note: All the waterway maps in this guide are drawn with north at the top of the page. Except where change of scale is noted, all maps are of the same scale, 1" to the mile.

Getting Started

Invitation

Come, find a quiet river or a mirrored lake. Learn to launch and paddle a canoe, and practice paddling until your canoe slices smoothly and elegantly through the water. Use your canoe as a way to discover remote places and hidden marshes with their birds and ducks and streamside flowers and shrubs.

Do not canoe alone. Beginning canoeing is best when it is a partnership, so start with someone who knows a bit about canoeing, someone who can drive to the places where you can launch your canoe. The Adirondacks is full of quiet ponds and streams; this guide will introduce you to many ponds as well as the streams and rivers. The guide also lists and describes briefly a number of places where you can practice canoeing. It concludes with information on longer canoe trips for the time when you have become a strong and accomplished paddler.

A guide for canoeing flatwater is very different from a guide for hiking or whitewater canoeing, where information about the route is critical. If you have basic canoeing skills, it is easy to follow rivers or streams once you are on them, as long as you are confident that the stretches you plan to canoe have only flatwater. Thus the descriptions are about where to start and end with additional details about what to look for and enjoy.

These adventures have been chosen because they present few if any problems for the beginner, young or old. The Adirondacks have several long, traditional routes that involve camping and longer carries. These, along with additional canoe lakes and some not-quite-flatwater trips, are depicted in *Adirondack Waterways*, published by the Adirondack Tourism Council, P. O. Box 2149, Plattsburgh, NY 12901. The advertisers who help support this free booklet include many outfitters, places to rent canoes, and guides who can help you start canoeing.

Safety

Flatwater canoeing is safe only if you
1) know how to swim,
2) always wear an **approved life jacket** or personal flotation device,
3) have practiced swimming with your life jacket on so you know how it feels to depend on it.

When you are paddling, it is best to wear an old pair of sneakers, ones that can get wet. You may need protection from something sharp when you step out of the canoe.
4) Always be sure someone knows where you are going and when you are expected back. If there are registration boxes at parking areas, be sure to sign in.
5) The trips described in this guide have been chosen for flatwater paddlers. They avoid stretches of **rapids**, places where the water falls sharply over rocks. *Use caution; every time this guide mentions rapids and you hear them ahead, that is your clue to turn around.*

Wind, waves, current, and logs fallen across the water can alter the flow of streams and ponds. Check conditions carefully before you start. *Do not attempt any other sections of streams and rivers described until you have had instruction in whitewater canoeing.*

Driving to lakes and rivers

This guide gives simple directions to the beginnings of the canoe trips described, usually from one direction only. Because you may choose different approach routes or because the routes may be quite complicated, your parents or companions ought also to have a good map or atlas of the Adirondacks. The most useful is DeLorme's *New York State Atlas and Gazetteer*. It shows the rivers as well as roads.

Adirondack Maps in Keene Valley produces an *Adirondack Canoe Map*. It features access to longer routes not covered in this guide and details the St. Regis Canoe Area. Adirondack North Country Association (ANCA) also produces a map that shows roads and state land areas. Other maps and brochures are listed on page 118.

You may want to have the United States Geological Survey maps for the areas you plan to canoe. These maps will tell you the names of many landmarks--like mountains or peninsulas--that you may see on your trips. However, all the sketch maps in this guide are based on those USGS maps, and despite their small scale, they show as accurately as the USGS maps the many twists and turns of these Adirondack waterways.

Your canoe

If someone in your family or a good friend has a canoe, you are indeed fortunate. If you have to rent a canoe to get started, there are several outfitters throughout the Adirondacks who rent canoes (see page 31). No matter which, you first need to become acquainted with your canoe.

A canoe has two seats, one in the front or **bow,** the other in the rear or **stern**. The seat in the stern is close to that end of the canoe; the seat in the bow is located far enough from the front so that you have room for your legs and feet. Most canoes are symmetrically shaped so that the only way to tell the bow from the stern is by the location of the seats. If you are sitting facing the bow, the **right side of the canoe** is on your right.

If you draw a line from the bow to the stern along the bottom of the canoe that line is called the **keel**. Some canoes have raised extensions along the keel-line.

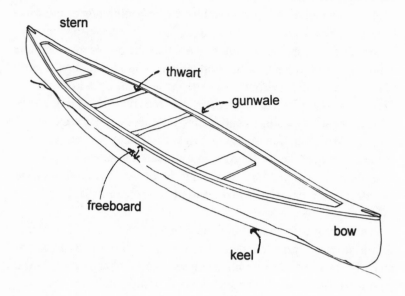

The tops of the sides of the canoe are called the **gunwales**. When a canoe is in the water, the distance from the waterline to the gunwale is known as the **freeboard**.

Canoes come in a wide variety of shapes, sizes, and materials. Try several before you and your family buy a canoe so you can be sure your canoe suits your needs. A longer, classic wooden canoe is great on open lakes, but too heavy to carry any distance.

A short, lightweight aluminum canoe is fine for twisting streams blocked by beaver dams and logs. You would need a very small, super-light canoe if you want to carry it to distant ponds. You may want to compromise on a canoe made of fiberglass or Kevlar that is rugged and relatively light. *Royalex*--heavier, durable, and scratch-resistant--is an affordable material that is popular in recreational canoes. Choose a canoe of medium length, around 15 to 16 feet, that is fairly streamlined, with an adequate freeboard. Your canoe should be wide enough to be relatively stable. No single design is best in all situations, so it is important to wait to make any decision until you have tried several different canoe styles under different conditions.

Your paddle

Paddles come in all sorts of shapes, but they all have the same basic features. The handle has a knob at the end so you can hold it with the best grip for pushing. The **blade** is the flat part that does the work in the water. The end of the blade can be either rounded or straight. Blades can be either wide or narrow. The **shaft** can be straight or bent in relation to the blade. With experience you will discover what type of paddle suits you best; to start just be sure the paddle is short enough so that you can comfortably reach between the **grip**, held in one hand, and the **throat** held in your other hand. Proper hand placement allows you to pull the blade through the water. The proper length for a straight-shaft paddle is the distance between the ground and your chin; for a bent-shaft paddle it is the distance between the ground and your chest.

grip   shaft   throat   blade   tip

Paddling is a partnership

Paddling alone can be fun, but it is much harder than paddling with a parent, grandparent, or older friend who has had experience with a canoe. When you are first learning, paddle in the bow, with your partner in the stern, so you can learn how to paddle straight ahead. As soon as you have managed that, try paddling from the stern. The stern paddler does most of the steering on open, calm water.

The bow paddler watches for obstacles, provides power, and sets the pace. The stern paddler steers the canoe, chooses sides to paddle on, and acts as captain.

To move along the most efficiently, both paddlers time their strokes together, paddling on opposite sides of the canoe. For the best paddling you and your partner should practice so you work as a team.

The bow or power stroke

With one hand on the grip and one hand on the throat of the paddle and your arms straight out, but not locked, reach ahead with the blade of your paddle. Pull with your lower arm and push with your upper arm. You have to turn as you do this in order to move your paddle in a straight line down the side of your canoe. Pull your paddle out, turning back as you do to reach out ahead and begin the next stroke. Most of the time you will use this power stroke.

Paddling straight ahead

If there is wind, waves, or even a slight current, or if the team's strokes are not balanced, the stern paddler will have to steer the canoe in order to keep it going straight ahead. There are two basic **steering strokes**. These strokes will keep your canoe on course without making it lose forward momentum, in other words continuing ahead as smoothly as possible.

Sweep stroke

Reach forward with your paddle, turn the blade out and pull the paddle back by rotating at your waist and tracing a half circle in the water with your paddle. Imagine that your seat is the center of the circle.

The sweep stroke is used to make big corrections in turning your canoe. It turns the bow of your canoe away from the side you are paddling on.

J stroke

Begin with the power stroke but, midway through, rotate the paddle by turning your body at your waist and pointing the thumb on your grip hand down toward the water. These moves rotate the blade. Next, your hand on the throat of the paddle smoothly pushes the paddle away from the canoe. When you are paddling on the left side of the canoe your blade traces a J in the water; the J is reversed when you paddle on the right.

The J stroke is used to make small corrections in turning the bow toward the same side you are paddling on.

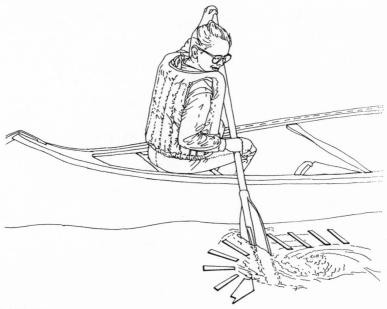

Switching sides

Practice paddling straight, with the bow paddler using power strokes and the stern paddler using steering strokes as needed. Paddlers should alternate the sides they paddle on regularly so they are less apt to get tired. But don't switch sides to steer. If you do, instead of going straight ahead, your canoe will zigzag through the water. Remember, both paddlers switch sides at the same time.

Other strokes

For turning quickly in current or to avoid logs and rocks in the water, you will need to know three more strokes. These strokes are used by both the bow and stern paddlers to make quick steering corrections.

Draw stroke

Turn the blade of your paddle parallel to the keel of the canoe. Reach out with the paddle and place the paddle straight up and down in the water. Pull the paddle toward the canoe.

The draw stroke is useful for changing course quickly. The bow paddler uses it to pull the bow away from an obstacle on the opposite side of the canoe.

Pry stroke

Turn the blade of your paddle parallel to the keel of the canoe. Slide the paddle into the water close to the canoe where you are sitting or kneeling. Pull your hand holding the grip toward you, while pushing the throat away with your other hand.

The pry will make a quick steering change to push the canoe away from an obstacle on that side of the canoe.

Back strokes

You can reverse any forward stroke by paddling backwards. Back strokes are valuable for very quick turns especially when there is current because they slow the boat. A **back power stroke** will quickly slow your canoe.

For a **reverse sweep**, begin by placing the paddle alongside the canoe with the blade out and behind where you are sitting or kneeling. Push with your hand on the throat while pulling with your hand on the grip to trace a half circle with your paddle. Imagine that your seat is center of the circle. Your canoe will quickly turn to the same side you are paddling on if you use a reverse sweep. This stroke is not recommended for normal steering as it takes away from your forward motion.

Practice draws and sweeps in combinations around a course of buoys. Try to paddle a complete circle without switching sides using a combination of strokes. Set up a zigzag course and practice coordinating tight turns using combinations of power, steering, and turning strokes.

Navigating narrow, twisting streams

Working together, the bow and stern paddler can use combinations of draw, pry, and reverse sweep strokes to turn quickly in moving water. You and your partner have to practice and communicate your moves to master these strokes.

Some of the streams described in the final chapter have a significant amount of moving water. They produce a **current** that keeps your canoe moving downstream even when you are not paddling. This guide suggests you canoe these streams downstream only, but you will have to be very adept at maneuvering your canoe quickly.

Even on a quiet stream, you may not see an underwater rock or log until you are almost upon it. A quick and coordinated response is important.

Suppose the stern paddler is paddling on the right and the bow paddler sees a rock close on the left. The stern paddler can quickly paddle backwards or tracing a backwards J while the bow paddler uses a pry stroke. This combination will move the bow to the right.

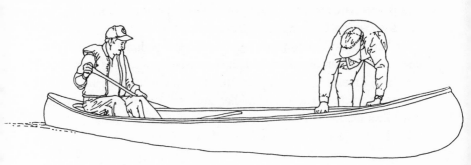

Where to start flatwater canoeing

You can begin to practice flatwater canoeing on lakes and ponds when there is little or no wind. It takes skill to manage a canoe in even a light wind. A flat section of a stream or river with little current is a good place to start, especially if the river is sheltered from the wind by hills or trees. Remember always practice with a partner, never alone.

The suggested lakes and ponds have fewer motorboats than some busy waterways. Practice well away from motorboat traffic until you are skilled enough to point your canoe at the line of waves those boats make.

Getting in and out of your canoe

The canoe is the most stable when it is completely on the water. To launch from shore, point the canoe into the lake. If the stern is closest to shore, the stern paddler steadies the canoe by placing it between his legs and holding it with both hands. The bow paddler then steps into the center of the canoe and moves forward keeping hands on the gunwales and the body bent and your weight low. The bow person then sits or kneels and steadies the canoe by bracing with the paddle while the stern paddler gets into the canoe. Always put your paddle down before moving around in the canoe.

When you are **getting out**, never run your canoe up on shore. Doing that reduces the life of your canoe and makes it unstable because the canoe is no longer floating.

When the bow is closest to shore, the bow paddler gets out first and holds the canoe with both hands, braced between his legs to steady it. The stern paddler then climbs through keeping his weight low and centered. The stern paddler should practice walking to the bow, keeping his body low, so this maneuver works safely.

Launching is easiest from a dock, with the canoe alongside. The stern paddler steadies the canoe until the bow paddler is safely seated, then gets in keeping the body balanced over the center of the canoe.

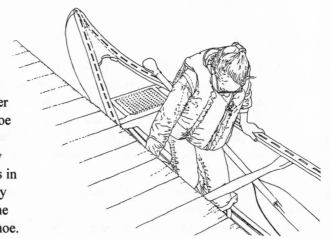

Tipping over

When you are canoeing on flatwater on calm days and observe the cautions above, you should not tip over. But, suppose something goes wrong; then you need to know what to do. The best way to find out what to do is to put on your bathing suit and visit one of the lakes mentioned in the guide and tip your canoe over and practice returning it to shore. Be sure you are with an experienced swimmer who is also an experienced canoeist.

The first thing you may notice when you try to tip your canoe over is that it is not a very easy thing to do. You and your partner may have to lean way out on one gunwale. However, some canoes are very tippy and finding out which ones are the most stable will help you decide what kind of canoe to use.

Remember, your canoe is designed to float. If you tip over, hold onto your canoe. If you can, swim it along to shore, pull it up on shore and dump the water out. Supposed it has tipped over and is upside down. You can right it while you are in the water so it is easier to maneuver. Never let go of the canoe--for your own safety.

Kneeling to paddle

For a long trip or for strong paddling against a wind or current, many paddlers find kneeling better than sitting. Also, with your weight low in this way, the canoe is more stable in high winds and waves. Even if you do not kneel all the time, it is often good to alternate between sitting down and kneeling so you will not get too tired on a long trip.

Put-in, take-out

Put-in is the way canoeists describe the place they start their trip. Some trips begin and end at the same launch site. Others have a different point of ending called the **take-out**.

Shuttle

The drive between put-in and take-out is called a **shuttle**. One-way directions for this drive are given in the last chapter where the put-in differs from the take-out.

Carrying a canoe

If you have to carry a canoe for a very short distance, you and your partner can hold an upright canoe from opposite sides.

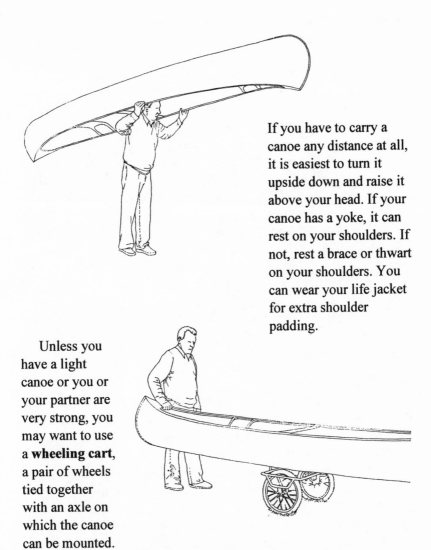

If you have to carry a canoe any distance at all, it is easiest to turn it upside down and raise it above your head. If your canoe has a yoke, it can rest on your shoulders. If not, rest a brace or thwart on your shoulders. You can wear your life jacket for extra shoulder padding.

Unless you have a light canoe or you or your partner are very strong, you may want to use a **wheeling cart**, a pair of wheels tied together with an axle on which the canoe can be mounted.

Carrying a canoe between canoeable or navigable waters is called a **portage**. Portages can be long or short. Wheeled carts work on trails designed as carries and for portages to remote lakes and ponds where the trails are suitably graded.

For the longest portages, you may want a very lightweight (as little as 15-pound) canoe that a single paddler can carry great distances. They are really great for the adventuring canoeist who wants to carry long distances to explore far-away ponds. You should become a good paddler before venturing out alone in such a canoe.

Car-top carrier

Your partner will need a **car-top carrier**. Two people, with practice, can easily lift a canoe, turn it upside down, and place it on the carrier. The important thing to remember is that you must secure the canoe with stout lines tied with proper knots. The bow and stern should be tied to the front and back of your car; lines or straps should wrap around the canoe and your carrier or the car-top itself.

For a light canoe, a carrier may not be needed. Foam blocks slipped over the gunwales will suffice; just be sure to attach all the lines.

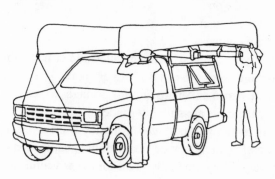

What you see when you are canoeing

Every stream is different, but there are many common features in our Adirondack waterways. Certain kinds of shrubs, trees, flowers, and ferns like the combination of sunlight, moisture, and wet soils found along the shores. Sheep laurel and pinxters bloom in spring along the edge of many ponds. Spireas--hardhack and meadowsweet--bloom at streamside in early summer. The white summer blossoms of elderberries tell you where to look in fall for their dark purple berries. Buttonbush follows in late summer with the brilliant colored blossoms of pickerelweed and cardinal flowers. The scarlet leaves of swamp maples are the first signs of autumn. They form a brilliant backdrop to the lavenders of asters and the golden shades of ferns touched by the first frost. The bright reds of American holly close out the fall season.

Expanses of reed beds border some streams. Fields of Joe-Pye weed turn marshes beside some streams pink in summer. The blossoms attract hordes of brilliant butterflies--you will soon recognize the red and white admirals, tiger swallowtails, and monarchs that flit among the flower-lined shores.

Some streams are bordered by dark evergreens, casting a deep gloom over the water. Overhanging silver maples make other waterways seem like secret tunnels.

Birds of all kinds like the edges between waterways and woods. Kingfishers are everywhere, their rattling call proceeding you downstream.

Sometimes you can glide quietly up to a heron standing still and watching for frogs and fish. Of the many ducks you see, wood ducks are the most colorful.

Unless you are canoeing at dawn or dusk, you may not spot many beaver, but you know from their dams and houses where they might be. It is rare to see an otter; muskrat are much more common. Occasionally, you may see a deer drinking from the stream. Bears are much less frequent, but in a summer of canoeing, you may see one at least.

Otter are rarely seen.

Best of all there is to enjoy on a flatwater canoe trip, I delight in the image of reflections on glassy, quiet water. White puffy clouds and blue sky create an upside-down world. The stumps and snags and upturned roots of trees killed by beaver dams are beautiful natural sculptures, whose intricate shapes are doubled when they are reflected. As your canoe breaks the water, the shimmering riffles turn the water's surface into a kaleidoscope of light and color. Flatwater canoeing is not a wild sport, but it is the finest way to get close to nature.

A few typical streamside plants and trees are illustrated in the guide; others are mentioned in the text. Flowers change between late spring and early fall, times you are most apt to be canoeing. Perhaps you would like to begin making a list of the different things you see on each trip.

Dragonflies and damselflies come in many bright colors--blues, greens, and reds.

Canoe Rentals, Outfitters, and Instructors

Tickner's Moose River Canoe Outfitters, Riverside Drive, Old Forge, 13420, is open from Memorial Day to Columbus Day. The proprietors, the Tickners, offer rental canoes, assistance with shuttles and advice on rivers in the area, 315-369-6286.

The Adirondack Scenic Railroad, which parallels the Moose River, plans to offer excursions in which you and your canoe can ride between navigable stretches of that river. They will do this in conjunction with Tickner's. The trips will start in Old Forge and end 0.5 mile north of Minnehaha, where the train will pick up canoes. Call 315-369-6290 for information.

Blue Mountain Outfitters, Box 144, Blue Mountain Lake, 12812, canoe rentals and guided trips, 518-352-7306

St. Regis Canoe Outfitters, Floodwood Road, Lake Clear, 12945, offers trip outfitting and instruction, 518-891-1838.

All Seasons Outfitters, 168 Lake Flower Ave., Saranac Lake, 12983, offers flatwater canoe lessons, whitewater canoe and kayak lessons, trip outfitting, guided trips, shuttle service, trip planning, and canoe and kayak rentals.

W.I.L.D./W.A.T.E.R.S., NY 28, The Glen, Warrensburg, 12885, offers canoe and kayak instruction for young people and adults, 518-494-7478.

Adirondack Professional Services and Outfitters, just west of Tupper Lake on NY 3, offers canoe and kayak rentals, 518-359-2174.

Most large lakes have boat liveries that rent canoes, paddles, and life jackets, too.

Many groups offer canoe workshops and instructions at different times: The Adirondack Mountain Club, Lake George, NY; chapters of the Red Cross; the American Canoe Association; and the Adirondack Park Visitor Interpretive Centers.

Easy Lakes and Ponds

This chapter contains some suggestions of places where you can begin learning to paddle your canoe. They were chosen because they offer a sample of the kinds of places you can visit with longer canoe trips. Pick places where you do not have to drive very far, because the practice ponds and lakes are quite small and do not offer the opportunities for exploring that are found in later chapters.

Wind and Waves

Start your canoeing adventures on a calm day so that you know how to handle your canoe before you meet a **headwind**, or wind coming from the direction you want to travel. There are times when Adirondack winds are so strong that you will have to pull your canoe ashore and wait for them to subside. In moderate **winds**, keep your canoe pointed directly upwind as much as possible to minimize the force of the wind on your canoe. When you meet high **waves** from wind or motorboats, point your canoe toward them; you can tip over if strong waves hit your boat broadside (sideways). When canoeing downwind in a strong wind, keep your canoe headed straight downwind, so the wind doesn't push the side of your canoe.

When you do reach shore, remember to pull your canoe far enough up on shore so wind and waves cannot carry it off. Then tie it securely to a tree or post.

Adirondack Map--
Campgrounds, Lakes, and Ponds

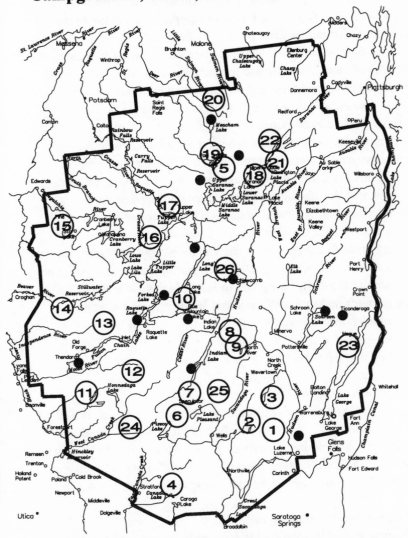

Campgrounds are indicated by a dot. Their descriptions are numbered and arranged according to region and access: Southeast, **1**; East of Northway, **2-4**; Central near NY 30 and 28N, **5-9**; West, near Old Forge and NY 28, **10-12**; and Northern, **13-15**.

Campgrounds

New York State's Department of Environmental Conservation (DEC) has some of the most beautiful campgrounds in the Eastern United States. Many of them have good boat launch sites. Reservations (1-800-456-CAMP) are needed if you wish to camp at them. All of them have day-use fees, but the following list gives a sample of fifteen campgrounds on smaller lakes where you can practice canoeing. A few have canoe and boat rentals, too.

Some of the campgrounds have inlets to explore and a few do not permit motorboats of any kind. The rest were included because they do not have heavy motorboat traffic. (The State campgrounds not listed in this book are on larger lakes where wind and motorboats may be a problem for the beginner.) Even on the lakes with recommended campgrounds, wind may be a problem for the beginner.

Campgrounds are open between Memorial Day and Labor Day; some stay open into October. Details of campgrounds and the other opportunities they offer are given in John Sheib's *State Parks and Campgrounds in Northern New York*, and Elizabeth Folwell's *The Adirondack Book*.

1. Luzerne Campground

Luzerne Campground is located on Fourth Lake, which is a small, man-made lake off NY 9N, north of Lake Luzerne. It is ideal for canoeing because no motorboats are allowed there. If there is enough water, you can paddle down the outlet of Fourth Lake through a chain of little lakes all the way to the town beach on Lake Luzerne.

2. Putnam Pond Campground

Putnam Pond Campground is accessible from a road that heads south of NY 74 closer to Ticonderoga than to Schroon Lake. Bays, a peninsula, and an island define quiet water for beginning canoeists. It's 2-mile length and irregular shore offer 5 miles of exploring by canoe.

3. Paradox Lake Campground

Paradox Lake Campground is north of NY 74. Route 74 heads east from the Northway just north of Schroon Lake. Paradox Lake is narrow with protected bays, one of which should be calm no matter the wind direction. The 4-mile long lake is so narrow a circuit of its shores hardly exceeds 8 miles of paddling.

4. Lincoln Pond Campground

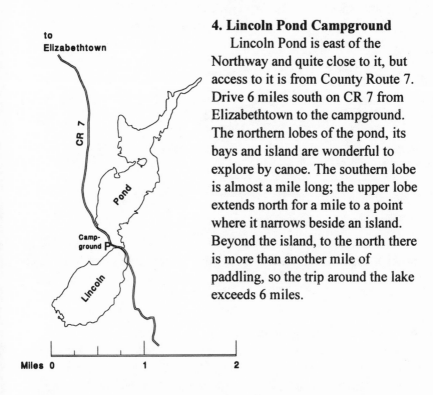

Lincoln Pond is east of the Northway and quite close to it, but access to it is from County Route 7. Drive 6 miles south on CR 7 from Elizabethtown to the campground. The northern lobes of the pond, its bays and island are wonderful to explore by canoe. The southern lobe is almost a mile long; the upper lobe extends north for a mile to a point where it narrows beside an island. Beyond the island, to the north there is more than another mile of paddling, so the trip around the lake exceeds 6 miles.

5. Lewey Lake Campground

Lewey Lake is 13 miles north of Speculator on NY 30 and 11 miles south of Indian Lake village. Protected by high mountains on the west and northwest, Lewey Lake is often calmer than nearby Indian Lake. Winds there can make Indian Lake too rough for even experienced canoeists. Marshes line the southern end of Lewey Lake 1.5 miles from the campground. The inlet, the Miami River, see page 62, is one of the region's best short stream paddles.

6. Lake Durant Campground

Lake Durant is a man-made lake created by a dam on the Rock River. The campground is on the west side of NY 30, just south of Blue Mountain Lake. Rock Lake is connected to the western end of Lake Durant and is very attractive. Much of Lake Durant's shoreline is filled with marsh plants and birds; herons and ducks abound. The canoeable waterway is almost 3 miles long.

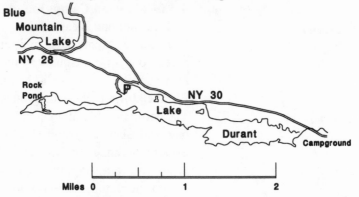

7. Forked Lake Campground

Forked Lake Campground offers canoe rentals. From Deerland, 3 miles south of Long Lake, drive southwest on North Point Road for 5 miles to a right fork to the campground. The lake stretches east-west for over 4 miles.

8. Lake Eaton Campground

Lake Eaton has bays that can be quiet depending on the direction of the wind. It is located just north of Long Lake Village off NY 30. Sandy swimming beaches surround the lake; you can reach them by canoe. The lake is 1.5 miles across at its widest so a circuit is about 4 miles long.

9. Lake Harris Campground

Lake Harris Campground is north of NY 28N in Newcomb, not far east of the Visitor Interpretive Center. You can paddle from the lake to the Hudson River and go a short way both up and downstream on the river. The lake is 2 miles long with a bay to the south and views north to the High Peaks.

34

10. Nicks Lake Campground

The access road to Nicks Lake Campground turns south from NY 28 near Thendara, 1.5 miles southwest of Old Forge. With many small bays and peninsulas, this is an ideal canoeing lake, especially as no motorboats are allowed. The lake is narrow with a twisting shoreline that offers only a 2.5-mile circuit. Rentals are available.

11. Limekiln Lake Campground

Limekiln Road heads south of NY 28 just east of Inlet and leads to the popular campground in 2 miles. Quiet bays set off by peninsulas and islands are found on the western and southern parts of the lake. With an irregular shape that is 1.4 miles across at its greatest, a circuit is not much over 3 miles.

12. Brown's Tract Ponds Campground

No motorboats are allowed on Brown's Tract Ponds, making them ideal for canoes. Lower Pond, 0.8 mile long, has a less developed wilderness campground, though plans to add showers and electricity may change that. Rental canoes are available. The campground is 2.3 miles west of Raquette Lake Road on Uncas Road. Canoe a 2.3-mile circuit or paddle to Lower Pond's island to swim and picnic there. Continue west on the on Uncas Road for 0.5 mile to even smaller Upper Pond, which is also good for canoes and is close to the road with a nice sandy beach.

13. Fish Creek and Rollins Pond Campgrounds

Both campgrounds have motorboat launch sites on their principal lakes. They are very popular and very crowded. However, they are the entrance points to a series of interconnected wilderness lakes and ponds. Practice on Fish Creek or one of the smaller ponds, like Whey Pond, which is accessible from the campground roads.

14. Meacham Lake Campground

Meacham Lake is east of NY 30 in the northern Adirondacks. Meacham Lake Road is 9.5 miles north of Paul Smiths. The lake is large (2 miles long and more than a mile wide) and exposed and not the best for beginner canoeists, but the southern end with marshes near both the outlet and inlet stream is fun to explore. The inlet, Osgood River, is canoeable for several miles upstream, south, see page 89.

15. Buck Pond Campground

Buck Pond Campground is in the northern Adirondacks, west of Paul Smiths and north of Onchiota. Follow signs from NY 192A and CR 30. Buck Pond is fairly small and protected. From canoe access to Lake Kushaqua, continue southwest through Kushaqua and Rainbow Narrows, see pages 65-66.

Ponds and Lakes

The smaller the lake or pond, the quieter it will be for canoeing. Many of those listed in this chapter are entirely or almost entirely surrounded by State land. Twenty of the twenty-four described have access from good highways. Few of them have developed boat launch sites, so you will have to practice getting in and out of your canoe under a variety of conditions. Every body of water is different with something new to discover while you are gaining confidence in paddling. Several of these also have inlets or outlets to explore.

Hardhack Spirea

The lakes are numbered and arranged according to region and access: Southeast, **1-3**; South, **4-6**; Central, **7-10**; West, **11-13**; Northwest, **14-15**; North, **16-20**; Northeast, **21**; and those with long dirt access roads, **22-25**.

1. Lens Lake

Lens Lake is one of the most accessible bogs in the Adirondacks. The eastern shore is privately owned, and access from the road is possible, although to be sure, ask permission. Heron nest at the northern end of the mile-long body of water, whose surface is almost half covered with thick mats of sphagnum, where sundew, pitcher plants and other typical **bog plants** grow.

Access is from Hadley Road in Stony Creek, west on Branch Road, then south on States Road to Lens Lake Road.

2. Harrisburg Lake

Harrisburg Road heads northwest from the settlement of Stony Creek, curves through west to southwest, and crosses a causeway that separates the northern portion of Harrisburg Lake from the swampy southern portion. The outlet, Stony Creek, flows south toward Northville. State land touches the lake to the west of the causeway.

The 1.5-mile long lake is only 0.6 mile wide at its broadest, but it is full of floating boggy masses, stumps, and wildlife.

Harrisburg Lake

to Stony Creek

P

Miles 0   1   2

3. Garnet Lake

Garnet Lake's northern shores are lined with private camps; its southern lobe is dotted with stumps and snags, water lilies and pond weeds, and it is a fine place to look for kingbirds.

to Johnsburg

P

Garnet Lake

The tall surrounding mountain peaks, dominated by Crane Mountain and Mount Blue, make it a very picturesque place to canoe. Drive south from Johnsburg and NY 8 on Garnet Lake Road. Follow signs to the lake and continue south on the road along the east shore for 0.5 mile to a small patch of state land, where you can park and launch a canoe. Paddle south for a mile to the narrows, then make a 1.5-mile circuit of the lower lobe before returning to the launch site.

Miles 0   1   2

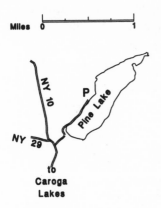

Miles 0 ____ 1

4. North End Pine Lake

Pine Lake has an amusement park on its southern shore. Its northern shoreline has quiet bays, twisted stumps, and water plants. Pine Lake is located at the intersection of NY 10 and 29A, north of Caroga Lakes. Follow the access road to the left around to the western shore of the lake. Just beyond the last camp there is a small parking area on state land and a good beach for launching your canoe. It is 0.75 to the end of the marshes.

5. Osgood Pond

The state has constructed a new canoe launch for Osgood Pond. Put-in here for a trip around the pond on a windless day or use it for described on page 112. There are camps around Osgood Pond, but much of the shoreline, especially along the outlet, is publicly owned.

Drive east from Paul Smiths on NY 86 for 0.6 mile and turn left on White Pine Road. The launch site (no camping) is 0.2 mile down that road. Near the end of the road is White Pine Camp, where for a fee you can tour one of the Adirondack's more unusual old camps.

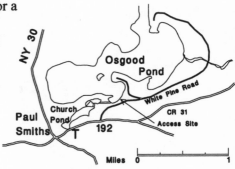

6. Oxbow Lake

Oxbow Lake is north of NY 8 and visible from it. The put-in is near the bridge over Oxbow Outlet. The bridge is a short distance along the road toward Piseco Airport from NY 8.

Launch beside the bridge, but park fifty feet farther west along the shoulder of the road. Oxbow Mountain looms over the southwest side of this long (1.7 miles), narrow body of water.

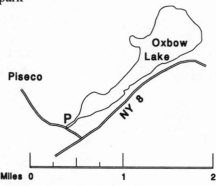

An **oxbow** is the U-shaped collar that is put around an ox's neck. Two oxbows are attached to a yoke in a pair to make a harness for a team of oxen. When a slow-moving stream wanders through a marsh, it often changes course, creating U-shaped loops also called oxbows. Many Adirondack flatwater streams have oxbows. Often while paddling you find yourself rounding a big loop and ending up within a few yards of the beginning of the oxbow. Oxbow Lake, however, does not have a shape that lives up to its name. Maybe it got its name from Oxbow Mountain, which does have the shape of an oxbow.

Notice that when you are paddling around a curve or oxbow, the water is deeper on the outside edge of the curve because the current is stronger. You often find sand bars too shallow for paddling on the inside edge of curves.

7. Mason Lake

Mason Lake is on the west side of NY 30, 8 miles north of Speculator and south of Lewey Lake Campground. Jessup River Road forks southeast from NY 30, 0.4 mile north of the highway's closest approach to the lake and follows the western shore of Mason Lake. Along this stretch of road there are several campsites and you can find an equal number of put-ins.

Mason Lake has beautiful, dark, evergreen-enclosed shores, islands, and tiny bays. It is very small, but a wonderful and very accessible place to explore by canoe.

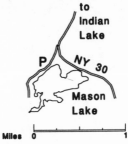

8. Lake Abanakee

Lake Abanakee is a widening of Indian River just below the outlet dam of Indian Lake. Access is from the parking turnout on the eastern end of the causeway that divides the lake. Drive 0.5 mile south of Indian Lake village on NY 30, turn left on Big Brook Road to the causeway.

Heading southeast, you can canoe almost to the rapids below Indian Lake Dam. In 0.7 mile, you pass a bridge over Jerry Savarie Road, and if you canoe under the bridge, you can explore the marshes surrounding Big Brook and the narrow channel of Round Pond Brook for nearly 2.5 miles more.

If you head north from the causeway, the lake is more open, with many more camps, then it narrows before reaching the NY 28 bridge, 2 miles northeast of the Big Brook Road causeway.

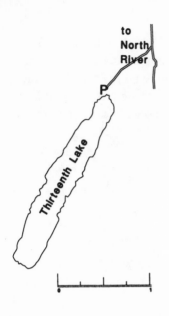

9. Thirteenth Lake

This lake is long and thin and lies in the northeast-southwest direction, typical of Adirondack **fault valleys** (valleys formed along a break in the underlying bedrock). Tall mountains ring both east and west shores. There is a public launch near the outlet at the north end. To reach it, drive southwest from North River on Thirteenth Lake Road, making a right fork at 3.5 miles and continuing to a parking area at the end of the road. There is a short (200 yard) carry to the lakeshore. Several beautiful wilderness campsites are located along both shores of the 2-mile-long lake, only a small part of which is private. The best campsites are on a peninsula 1.4 miles from the launch site.

10. South Pond

South Pond is very popular. It has a few private homes on the northern shore, but most of the shoreline is **Forest Preserve** or land owned by the State. It is a fairly large body of water, a rough triangle shape a mile on a side, so wind can be a problem. There are rocky islands with nesting gulls, sandy beaches for swimming, islands and bays to explore, and an osprey nest to observe from a distance. Visiting the islands and circling the pond add up to almost 5 miles of canoeing.

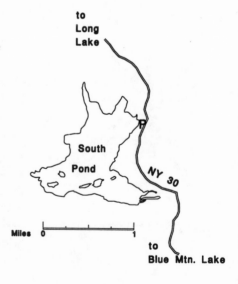

The parking area for South Pond is on the west side of NY 30, 5.9 miles north of Blue Mountain Lake. On the north side of the parking area a wide trail leads 100 yards down to shoreline.

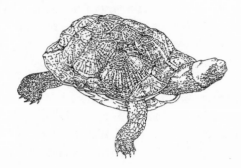

11. North Lake

North Lake is almost 3.5 miles long, very thin, with so many bays you can paddle more than 8 miles to explore its circumference. Its northern shores are part of newly acquired easement lands. (The state has acquired an **easement** or agreement that gives public access and other rights, while the owner retains the right to log the land.) You can drive along the road that follows the western shore. It passes several campsites and places to launch your canoe.

From NY 28, north of Alder Creek, turn east following signs to Forestport Station and continue northeast on North Lake Road. That road stretches northeast for nearly 15 miles to the outlet of North Lake. Just before the dam at the outlet, the west shore road forks left.

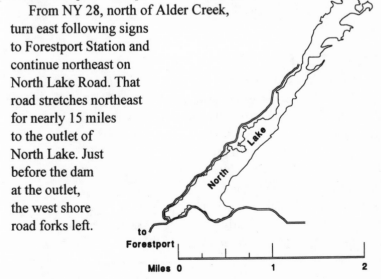

12. Ponds in the Moose River Plains

Dirt roads lead close to several of the small ponds in the Moose River Plains. The Plains Road (additional descriptions in DEC brochure, *Moose River Recreation Area*, and *Discover the West-Central Adirondacks*) is a 22-mile connector between the end of Cedar River Road southwest of Indian Lake Village and Limekiln Road south of Inlet. Both accesses are from NY 28 in the middle of the Adirondack Park. The long dirt road has many points of interest; the most accessible canoe ponds are Lost Ponds and Indian Lake. Lost Ponds are a widening of Sumner Stream. A dirt road leading to them forks north from the Plains Road, 2 miles east of the T intersection of Limekiln and the Plains roads, 11.65 miles west of the entrance to the Plains near Wakely Dam on Cedar River. You have to carry your canoe 0.4 mile from the parking area at the end of the dirt road.

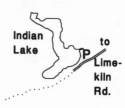

To find Indian Lake, turn south from the T in the Plains and follow the road almost to its end. The closest the road comes to Indian Lake is 200 yards and there are only unmarked paths leading to it, not marked trails. However, it is an easy carry and a wonderful wilderness lake to explore, with an osprey nest on an island near the north end.

13. Moss Lake

Moss Lake is a short distance from a good parking area on Big Moose Road. Big Moose Road heads north from NY 28 in Eagle Bay for 2.1 miles to the parking are which is on the west, left.

Osprey have been sighted here. The lake has good swimming; you might want use this spot to practice tipping your canoe over, righting it, and getting it to shore. (Camping here is by permit only.) The irregularly shaped lake is 0.7 mile across at its widest.

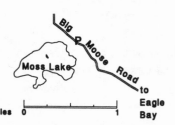

14. Francis Lake

Francis Lake is one of the best to explore by canoe, although it takes a long drive to get there from either of the two access roads. It is small, only 0.75 mile long, but with all the bays and eskers to explore, you will paddle more than a 3-mile circuit.

From the south and east, drive north on Big Moose Road and continue on Stillwater Road to a T intersection. Stillwater Lake is a right turn. Take Number Four Road to the west, left, for approximately 6 miles to Francis Lake. You will pass three dirt roads that fork north. Park just beyond the third. Francis Lake is 175 feet to the south from the road. Alternatively, drive east of Lowville on Number Four Road to the settlement of Number Four and turn right. Blacktop ends in 0.45 mile, the foot trail to the northern tip of the lake is at 0.85 mile, parking is just beyond.

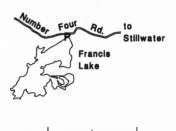

Tall pines surround the lake; ravens are often found in them. The lake has a number of lobes and bays, pine-covered islands, eskers, and peninsulas, and many places to explore in several hours of quiet canoeing. The southeastern lobe seems especially remote.

An **esker** is a twisted ridge of sand and gravel. Sometimes these ridges wind through flatlands for several miles. They can be 200 feet tall, with steeply sloped sides. Eskers were deposited by glacial meltwater flowing under retreating glaciers. You can often see such ridges while you are canoeing on ponds and streams in the flat sandy plains that were created by glacial lakes. Pine trees, which grow best in sandy, gravely soil are often found on the slopes of eskers.

15. Streeter Lake

Streeter Lake is a small, **boreal** lake, a northern lake whose shores are typically bordered with balsam and spruce. The lake measures less than 0.5-mile across in any direction. The launch site for canoeing around the lake is at the end of the Aldrich-Streeter Lake Road, 4.4 miles south of the barrier at the entrance to the Aldrich Wild Forest.

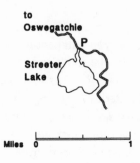

To find that entrance, drive west of Star Lake on NY 3, turn south toward Oswegatchie (0 mile). Turn left at the first intersection, then right at about 1 mile (before you cross the railroad tracks) onto Coffin Mills Road. Pass Coffin Mills at 2.2 miles and Aldrich at 4 miles. Turn left at 4.3 miles just before the barrier that marks the entrance to Aldrich Pond Wild Forest.

16. Horseshoe Lake

Horseshoe Lake is a large lake, almost entirely surrounded by Forest Preserve land. It is shaped like a fat L, and each arm is a mile long so it may prove too exposed for canoe practice. It is a great place to fish and enjoy an evening paddle when the wind has dropped.

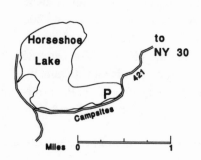

Drive west on NY 421 from NY 30 south of Tupper Lake. At 1.6 miles, the road makes a sharp turn to the right. Continue to the south shore of Horseshoe Lake, which is 4.7 miles from NY 30. There are numbered campsites on sandy beaches on the south shore, good places to launch a canoe.

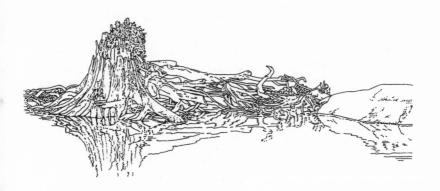

17. Piercefield Flow

Piercefield Flow is a widening of the Raquette River downstream from the outlet of Raquette Pond, which, in turn, is a northern lobe of Tupper Lake. Access is from NY 3 in Piercefield, west of Tupper Lake village. Launch south of the bridge over the Raquette River. Niagara Mohawk Power Corporation has provided parking and the flow stretches 2.3 miles upstream from the bridge. Dotted with stumps and **snags** (broken trees or limbs rising from the bottom), the flow is a good place for viewing birds and fishing.

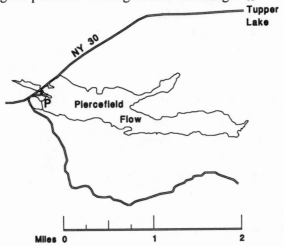

18. Moose Pond

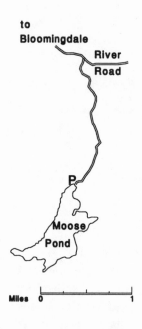

to Bloomingdale

River Road

P

Moose Pond

Miles 0 ⊢———————————⊣ 1

Moose Pond is a very handsome pond with bays and peninsulas overshadowed by the peaks of the McKenzie Mountain Wilderness Area. It is also a good fishing pond stocked by the state. A 2-mile paddle will take you around its circumference.

You can drive to the northern shore to launch a canoe there. Drive north of Saranac Lake to Bloomingdale on NY 3, which makes a sharp right-angle turn in Bloomingdale. Turn right 0.15 mile beyond that turn onto River Road and follow it for 1.65 miles to an unmarked right turn, which is Moose Pond Road. The pond is just short of 2 miles south of this intersection.

19. Black Pond and Long Pond

There is a wonderful, tiny canoe pond (only 0.7 mile long) not far from the Paul Smiths Visitor Interpretive Center. From it you can look north to Jenkins Mountain or south to St. Regis Mountain. Black Pond and adjacent Long Pond lie on land owned by Paul Smith's College. You can paddle around Black Pond, explore its eastern lobe, then paddle to the north end where a short (0.2-mile) carry will let you canoe Long Pond as well. Long Pond is a teardrop, half as long as Black.

Meadowsweet Spirea

Drive 2.5 miles west of Paul Smiths on Keese Mill Road. There is a church on the south side of the road. On the north, just beyond a stream is a small parking area. Walk north 200 feet to a dock on the outlet stream and paddle on into Black Pond.

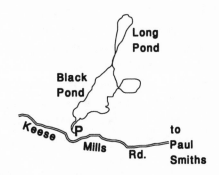

(Note that Black Pond and Long Pond are shown in a larger scale than other ponds. The scale was changed because the ponds are so small.)

20. Deer River Flow

Deer River Flow is a dark body of water in a dammed portion of the Deer River. Like many Adirondack ponds and many slow-moving streams, the water here is colored murky brown by the natural decaying of plants and trees. Fast-moving Adirondack waters are generally clear, unless they drain large boggy areas, and then they, too, can be stained dark brown.

There are few camps on the flow. Lots of stumps and snags to dot the flow or hide just under its surface. Launch beside the NY 30 bridge that a little less than 15 miles north of Paul Smiths. The flow is 2.5 miles long, but if you explore the inlet bay to the north you can paddle for 6 or more miles.

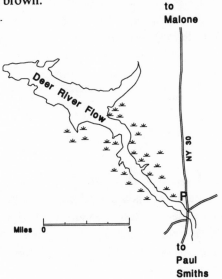

49

21. Franklin Falls Pond

Franklin Falls is a narrow lake created by a dam on the Saranac River. With three islands, several bays, views of Moose and Whiteface mountains, much state-owned and attractively wooded shoreline, and relatively little development on the rest, the pond (or reservoir) is a quiet place for paddling. Motorboats are limited to 10 horsepower. Winds can be strong because the pond has a northeast-southwest orientation. The southern, narrower end of the pond is calmer.

A 7-mile circuit of the pond, its inlet, and bays takes a half-day or so. Launch from the Niagara Mohawk Power Corporation (NIMO) car-top launch site beside the bridge where County Route 18 crosses the outlet, near the power dam.

There is also a small DEC parking area 2.4 miles southwest of the dam, near the southern end of the pond. This is within 0.5 mile of the end of the lake and a better launch when it is windy. From the DEC launch it is 0.5 mile west to the beautiful cascades of the Saranac River that drop into the deep pool that marks the beginning of the 2.8-mile long reservoir.

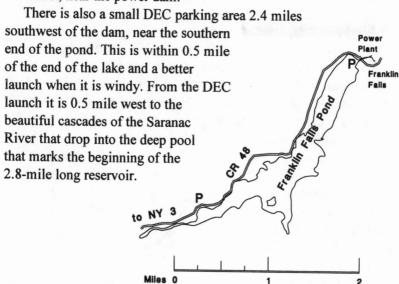

22. Union Falls Pond

Union Falls is 6 miles long, more than twice as long as Franklin Falls Reservoir, long enough that exploring the entire lake would benefit from having cars at either end. The wide open water can have whitecaps on windy days, but the narrower southern end is a flooded and much more scenic stream channel. You pass emerged stumps and weed beds and often see bald eagles which nest nearby.

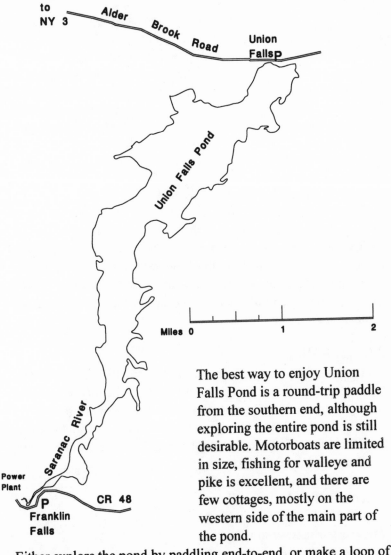

The best way to enjoy Union Falls Pond is a round-trip paddle from the southern end, although exploring the entire pond is still desirable. Motorboats are limited in size, fishing for walleye and pike is excellent, and there are few cottages, mostly on the western side of the main part of the pond.

Either explore the pond by paddling end-to-end, or make a loop of similar distance, 6 miles, from the southwestern launch site, which is on County Route 18, 300 yards north of the bridge and dam over the Saranac at the foot of Franklin Falls Pond. The northern launch is a NIMO car-top site off Alder Brook Road, just past and to the left side of the power dam at the foot of the lake.

At the End of Long Dirt Roads

Long, dirt roads that can be challenges to drive limit the number of people who visit the ponds at the end of long dirt roads. If your family has access to four-wheel-drive vehicle you can visit three of these ponds, which will seem much wilder and more remote than other, more accessible ponds. The fourth, Newcomb Lake, has a good road, but you have to hire a horse and cart to carry your canoe as no vehicles are allowed.

23. Jabe Pond

To make the pond accessible to fishermen DEC allows driving on the road to Jabe Pond, though often it appears the road is too rough for regular cars. Split Rock Road climbs steeply uphill from NY 9N near the shores of Lake George. It is the second road south of Hague. Jabe Pond Road forks left, south, from it, 1.8 miles from NY 9N.

The pond has several lobes and an island, and is popular with fishermen. It is almost a mile long, 0.6 mile wide at its widest. The evergreen-covered island is near the southern end.

Split Rock Rd.

to NY 9N

Miles 0   1

P

Jabe Pond

24. G Lake

A 3-mile-long, four-wheel-drive road heads north from NY 8 almost to G Lake, a small, odd-shaped lake that is best explored by canoe. The road is hard to spot from NY 8; it begins at the line between the Hamilton County towns of Piseco and Morehouse, about 5 miles east of Hoffmeister, 3 miles west of NY 8's intersection with Piseco's West Shore Road. The lake is a triangle, 0.5 mile on a side, with a deep peninsula nearly cutting it in two.

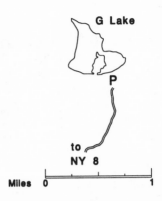

Note scale change

25. Upper Kunjamuk

The Upper Kunjamuk has muskrats and kingbirds, marsh hawks and sometimes heron, pond weeds and stumps. A small pond, less than a mile long, has been created by a fish barrier dam across the Kunjamuk River. It is on state land, but access is through International Paper Company's Speculator Tree Farm.

You can drive East Road off NY 30 north of Speculator to its end, 100 yards from the dam, without a permit. (You cannot stop at any other part of the tree farm without a permit.) The 8-mile drive on the dirt road is so slow that it sometimes takes an hour. At an intersection 0.2 mile from the end of the road, turn right or east, for 0.4 mile to a parking area. Carry around the gate to the river just above the dam. You can paddle a 2.5 mile circuit around the man-made pond.

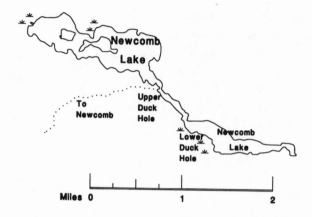

Miles 0   1   2

26. Newcomb Lake (with horse portage)

You cannot drive to the shores of Newcomb Lake and the access road/trail is 6 miles long, too long for carrying a canoe. However, you can hire a horse-drawn cart to transport your canoe to the lake. This is ideal if you wish to camp near the lakeshore and explore the lake and its islands by canoe. Santanoni Mountain looms over the lake. The northeast shore has cedar-ringed sandy beaches and there are two lean-tos, one on the south shore, the other on the northwest shore. You can also paddle around the wide sections of the outlet called Upper and Lower Duck Holes. Both Newcomb Lake itself and the Duck Holes are 1.5 miles long. Circling either of them is a trip of over 3.5 miles, so you can anticipate 7 or 8 beautiful miles of canoeing.

For a very special treat, your family will enjoy hiring one of the two outfitters in Newcomb: Ken Helms, Jr., 518-582-4191, and Tom Dillon, 518-582-2412. Newcomb is located on NY 28N, almost 14 miles east of Long Lake, 23.5 miles west of Exit 30 on the Northway. While you are at Newcomb Lake, take time to visit Camp Santanoni.

The access roadway leads to a bridge over the outlet of Newcomb Lake. Launch your canoe here. The continuing road leads across the bridge and northwest to Camp Santanoni, which is on a peninsula.

Streams with One Put-in

Streams with one put-in are great fun. These shorter trips are possible because the streams described have little current; you can go upstream or downstream with similar effort. There are often several channels and numerous bays and backwaters, so you have to learn to read the river to determine which way it is flowing. The easiest way--unless there is an obvious current--is to notice that grasses growing underwater point downstream.

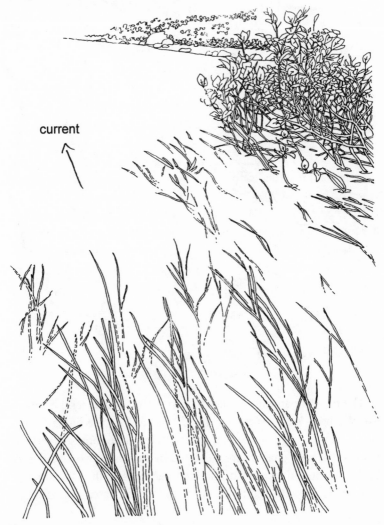

current

Adirondack Map--Streams with One Put-in

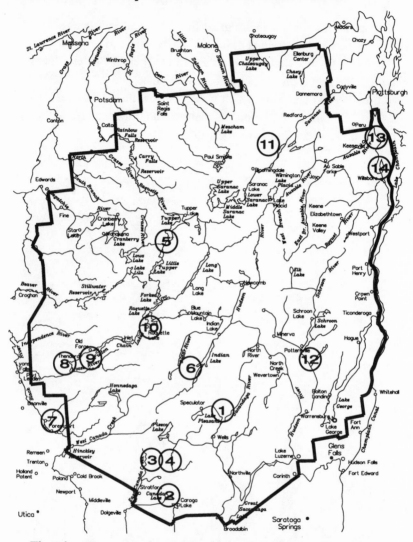

The trips are arranged according to region and access: Southern, **1-6**; Western, **7-10**; Northern, **11-12**; and two on the far eastern border of the Park. Notice that most of the canoe routes described in this and the next chapter are clustered in the south, west, and north. That is because the rivers of the east, particularly the Hudson and its tributaries, are wild and tumbling with few flatwater stretches.

Beaver Dams

Because these streams are so sluggish they are often dammed by beavers, so you will have plenty of practice carrying over beaver dams. If the shoreline beside the beaver dam is relatively dry and open, get out there and carry the canoe beyond the dam. However, beaver dams are rarely placed between dry points. If the dam seems dry and substantial, place your canoe parallel to the dam and get out, stern paddler first, just as if you were going ashore. Lift the canoe over and launch again.

If it is a typical dam, with deep water below and above, and branches sticking out in all directions, particularly downstream, it will take some careful maneuvering to get over it without tipping. Put the bow so that it is barely on the dam. If you pull it up too far and the bow paddler gets out, the stern paddler may sink or the canoe will tip because it is unstable. The bow paddler can get out on the dam without getting more than his or her sneaks wet. Then the stern

paddler moves very carefully forward to get out while bending low and grasping the gunwales to keep steady. You can brace your paddle against the gunwales for extra stability. Then you both lift the canoe over the dam. You have to be just as careful getting back in, only this time the bow paddler goes first, moving carefully along to the bow seat.

1. Auger Flats

Auger Flats on the Main Branch of the Sacandaga River may just be one of the best short canoe trips in the Adirondacks. The stream has a canopy of tall silver maples that reflect in its quiet waters. Rose-breasted grosbeaks nest in the low trees along the shoreline. Depending on beaver activity, there is a 2-mile canoeable stretch upstream. With the return, you will spend as little as two hours on the river. *Note: do not canoe downstream from the put-in. That way is very dangerous for it quickly leads to Auger Falls.* A path from the parking area leads to the falls. If you follow it, be very cautious and stay back from the steep slopes above the falls.

To find the launch site, drive north on NY 30 and 8 from the intersection of those two roads north of Wells. A dirt road heads right 1.5 miles north of that intersection. Follow the road 200 yards to the left almost to a beach launch spot beside the river.

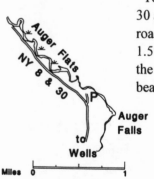

Silver maple

2. West Lake to Canada Lake

A good boat launch site that you will have to share with motorboats leads into West Lake, which is a part of Canada Lake, in the southern Adirondacks. Turn left from NY 10 and 29A on West Lake Road north of Canada Lake. Then turn immediately right for 0.3 mile to the parking area and launch dock. The channel winds and twists for almost 0.5 mile to West Lake. Depending on wind and waves, you can paddle to the marshes at the west end of West Lake or paddle south into Canada Lake, around Dolgeville Point, and southwest for to the channel that leads into Lily Lake. A circuit of that lake adds up to a 4-mile round-trip from the launch site. See map page 71.

3. East Canada Creek

The quiet section of the East Canada Creek near Powley Place is gem of a canoe trip, short, but very nice. Drive north on the Powley-Piseco Road from Stratford for almost 11 miles, or south for 8.2 miles on the same road from its intersection with NY 10, south of Piseco. There you will find an old iron bridge over a small stream beside a wide natural meadow. Park south of the bridge, launch your canoe on the east side of the bridge (it is not an easy launch-site).

You can canoe only briefly upstream before low-hanging alders stop you. Paddling downstream for almost 2 miles, you can enjoy elderberry bushes, ferns and frogs, and beautiful reflections along the quiet stream before you reach rapids. Turn around there. With the return, you can spend two or three hours exploring the river's meanders through the marshes.

Meander - Meander means to follow a winding or twisting course. The word came from a river with that name in western Turkey that is notable for its meandering way.

A typical Adirondack flatwater stream, meandering along, creating oxbows as it cuts through marshes.

4. West Branch Sacandaga River

A section of the headwaters of the West Branch of the Sacandaga River winds along beside NY 10 in southern Hamilton County. It offers three excellent canoeing opportunities from the one put-in, plus a marvelous shuttle trip, see page 102. Part of the time the north-flowing river is close to the highway, but you are rarely aware of its presence. Tall mountains line both sides of the valley, which is often very wide with the river meandering through its marshes. The quiet is very special and this is perhaps the best flatwater canoe stretch in the Adirondacks.

Two highway bridges cross the West Branch and you can put in at either. However the best launch site and parking area is adjacent to the second bridge north of Pine Lake. Drive 6 miles north of the intersection of NY 29A and 10 on NY 10 to the second bridge. Park either near the river or a hundred yards north at a marked turnout.

Upstream

Paddling upstream from the second bridge, you pass the entrance to Good Luck Lake, then swing back toward the road before beginning a wide arc east to the first bridge, 1.3 miles away. Overhanging trees make picturesque reflections. The stream seems dark and quiet. The trip is less than 2 miles, one way.

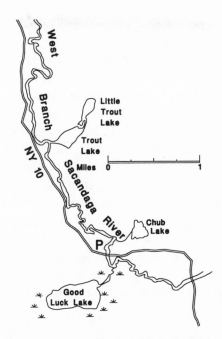

Good Luck Lake

If you turn west into Good Luck Lake through the pickerel weed growing in its outlet, you can extend the trip upstream by 2 miles exploring that lake's shores.

Trout Lakes

Heading downstream from the second bridge, you may not even notice where the tiny outlet of Chub Lake flows in on the right. If you can find it, and can carry over the beaver dams and obstructions, you can explore the unusual plant life of its bog-ringed shores. In late autumn you can pick wild cranberries.

Continuing north on the West Branch, watch as you approach Trout Lake Mountain, about a mile from the start. Another small stream also flows in on the right. If the water level permits, you can canoe up it to explore its hidden marshes. Then continue north to the entrance to Trout Lakes, 2 miles from the start. Paddle northeast through Trout to Little Trout, whose far shore is 0.7 mile from the West Branch. This trip and return offers 5.4 miles of paddling.

These three trips on the West Branch of the Sacandaga add up to 12 miles, so you may want to do them on at least two different days.

5. Above Bog River Falls

Immediately before the Bog River flows into South Bay of Tupper Lake it spills over a lovely waterfall. The waterfall is close to county route 421 and just under 0.5 mile from NY 30. The falls and the pools below and above make this a popular picnicking and swimming spot. There is room to park and an outhouse just down the road from the falls. Carry your canoe along a narrow path for 100 feet to quiet water above the falls.

From here you can enjoy a short, 1 1/2 hour, secluded flatwater trip, 1.6 miles upstream to the confluence of Bog River and Round Lake Stream. Just above the confluence rapids block both streams, so you will want to turn around and return to the take-out just above the falls.

6. Miami River from Lewey Lake

Head south from Lewey Lake Campground, page 33. The place where the Miami River empties into Lewey Lake is almost hidden in the marshes that border the south end of the lake. The mouth of the river is toward the western side of those marshes, about 1.3 miles from the launch site. The river winds south through the marshes, and with all

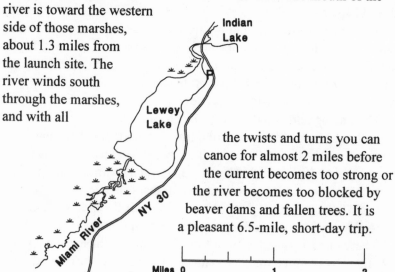

the twists and turns you can canoe for almost 2 miles before the current becomes too strong or the river becomes too blocked by beaver dams and fallen trees. It is a pleasant 6.5-mile, short-day trip.

7. Black River above Kayuta Lake

A 3-mile section of the Black River above Kayuta Lake is canoeable as far as Crandalls Falls. Here the river winds and twists south of Tamarack Swamp. There are a few summer camps, but most of the shoreline is a broad expanse of marsh bordered with tamaracks and other conifers.

To reach the launch for the upstream portion, drive east on Dayton Road to Bardwell Mill. Continue for 0.8 mile to a T where you turn left on Julia Road for 0.7 mile to a bridge over the Black. Launch from the northwest side of the bridge.

You can extend a canoe trip here by paddling northeast on Kayuta Lake, which is a dammed portion of the Black River. Motorboats are common here. With two cars you can canoe all the way to State Dam, where a launch site has been constructed at the end of State Dam Road. That road turns east, immediately north of the intersection of NY 12 and NY 28.

This long canoe trip takes you under the railroad bridge at 1.5 miles, under Dustin Road at 2.4 miles, past the confluence with Woodhull Creek, which can be explored for a short distance, to the dam at 3.3 miles, where there is a carry to 1.6-mile long Forestport Reservoir.

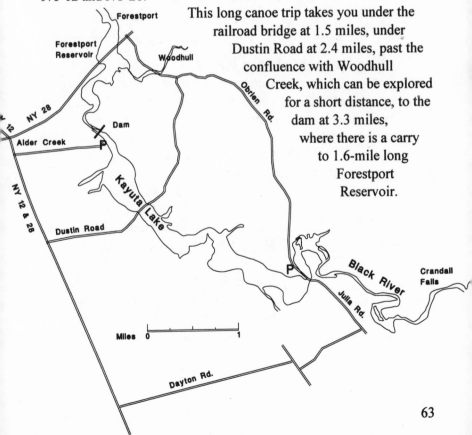

8. Main Branch Moose River to Nelson Lake

A short carry and a short trip down the Moose River will take you into Nelson Lake. DEC has recently designated a parking area on an old road that forks right, east, from NY 28, 2.8 miles north of the bridge at McKeever. There is a parking area not far from the highway. The old road is gated and you have to carry to the river. Stay left for 0.3 miles until the road crosses the railroad tracks. Across the tracks, the way left leads to Nelson Falls; the way straight ahead leads to the river in a calm section below the rapids.

Launch here and canoe downstream for a half mile, just short of the next rapids where the river bends. Follow calm water to the left into the channel that leads a quarter mile to Nelson Lake. A trip on the river with a circuit of the lake adds up to about 3.5 miles of paddling altogether, a half-day outing.

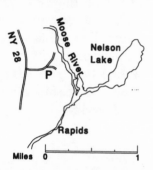

9. Middle Branch Moose River

Near Thendara there is a stretch of 1.2 miles of good flatwater canoeing on the Middle Branch of the Moose. Between the put-in and the wooden dam where you have to turn back, the river winds and turns through marshes and around islands, sheltered by a small hill to the northwest. The circuit of 2.5 mile down and back is good paddling practice in a pretty setting.

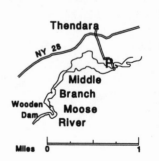

To find the launch site from the Thendara railroad station on NY 28, head east for 0.35 mile and turn right on Beech Street. Beech Street curves left, then right before crossing the bridge over the Middle Branch 0.4 mile from NY 28. Park to the right after you cross the bridge. The easiest put-in is on the northeast side of the bridge.

10. South Inlet, Raquette Lake

South Inlet is a special place for birds and ducks. The inlet stretches southwest from the shores of Raquette Lake for over 2 miles to a waterfall on the stream that drains Sagamore Lake. Access is very easy; launch on the south side of NY 28 just east of the bridge over the inlet. The bridge is obvious whether you are driving east from Raquette Lake Road or west from the turn to Golden Beach Campground. The knoll behind the launch site is covered with a virgin stand of red pines. Pines, hemlocks, balsams, and tamarack border the marshes that surround the inlet.

Allow two or three hours to enjoy the surroundings as you paddle along upstream to the waterfall and back. Motorboats and jet skis have begun to use the inlet, disturbing wildlife and paddlers, so spring and fall are good times to explore it.

11. North Branch Saranac River

This short stretch of river can be reached from Buck Pond Campground, page 36, by launching on Lake Kushaqua, and paddling southwest through Kushaqua Narrows under the bridge to Rainbow Narrows. The North Branch forks north, right, just out of sight of this bridge. Alternatively you can launch near that bridge. The bridge is on Mud Pond Road, which heads north

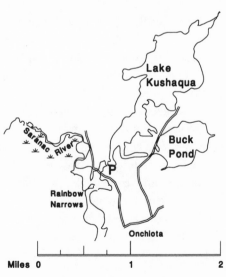

from Onchiota; it is also known as the back road to White Fathers. The North Branch of the Saranac has a broad flow near its confluence with the Saranac. Paddle north through this dark expanse of water, made even darker by surrounding evergreens. Near the head of the flowed area a small stream enters on the left. You have to paddle hard to go up a short stretch of riffles. You also have to carry over several beaver dams in order to explore the river's marshes all the way to private land about 2 miles from the bridge. Return to your launch site after paddling two to three hours from the bridge; add another hour or so if you started at Buck Pond Campground.

From Buck Pond launch, it is 1.2 miles to the bridge, another mile to the point the North Branch narrows, then 1.5 miles more upriver, depending on the beaver dams.

12. Schroon River just below Schroon Lake

Much of the Schroon River is full of rapids. One exception is a 4-mile stretch south of Schroon Lake. Flatwater ends at the Starbuckville Bridge and you can canoe this with a two-car shuttle, but the take-out above the bridge can be difficult in high water. It is better to explore the marshes just south of the lake and canoe as far as you want, returning to the put-in, which is a developed DEC launch site with good parking.

Turn east from NY 9 just north of Pottersville on the road marked Word of Life Camp. The launch site is 0.7 mile down this road.

From the launch, head south under the bridge, past islands and bays, to where Trout Brook flows in on the right. Head up it to explore a quiet stretch of brook with a canopy of silver maples. This detour is about 1.5 miles round-trip.

Be very cautious and make sure you can paddle back up the main stream before continuing on. In high water the river has a strong current here. Almost halfway to Starbuckville, the Schroon River circles around part of Jenks Swamp where you will find good birding. Camps line the lower portion of the river; if you plan to go on to Starbuckville take-out, stay left as you approach the bridge and the dam. The take-out is close to the bridge; do not go any closer to the dam. The current makes this a very dangerous place.

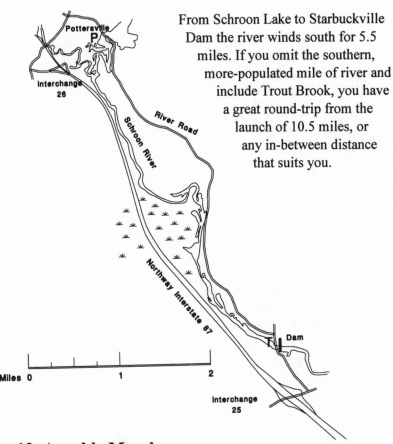

From Schroon Lake to Starbuckville Dam the river winds south for 5.5 miles. If you omit the southern, more-populated mile of river and include Trout Brook, you have a great round-trip from the launch of 10.5 miles, or any in-between distance that suits you.

13. Ausable Marsh

The twin mouths of the Ausable River enclose a broad marsh on the shore of Lake Champlain. Ausable Marsh is a wonderful place to canoe, with waterfowl, reed beds, wildflowers, and twisted watercourses. The marsh is 9 miles south of Plattsburgh. There are several ways to enjoy the marsh, but your choice depends on the wind and waves on Lake Champlain. You can put in at the beach in Ausable Campground and paddle upriver to NY 9. On the way back, you can take the south fork of the river and return along the shore of Lake Champlain, if it is calm enough. In between the two branches there is another channel through which to explore the marsh. The mouth of this channel is immediately south of the northern branch

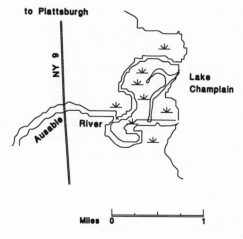

to Plattsburgh

NY 9

Lake
Champlain

Ausable River

Miles 0 ————————— 1

and the marsh beside the channel are even more varied than those by the river itself. In addition, if the lake is calm enough, it is possible to canoe north along the shore from the northern mouth of the Ausable to another quiet channel in the marsh.

If you paddle all the channels and lakeshores described, you could canoe nearly 10 miles.

14. Mouth of Boquet River

A 2-mile stretch of the Boquet is canoeable flatwater between Willsboro and Lake Champlain. The river is shallow and slow moving and full of ducks. The shores are privately owned, but a sandbar in the mouth is publicly owned, a good place for a picnic. The first settlement on the shores of Lake Champlain between Crown Point and Canada was built by in 1765 near the mouth of the Boquet.

The 4.2-mile round-trip can be made in 2 hours. Southeast of the NY 22 bridge over the Boquet, a road heads east beside the river. Follow it past the falls to a right fork that ends at the river, below the rapids, where you can launch your canoe.

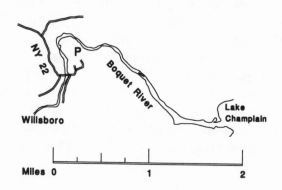

NY 22   P   Boquet River   Lake Champlain

Willsboro

Miles 0 —————— 1 —————— 2

Longer Trips with One Put-in

The longer trips with one put-in are often on rivers and streams with a slight current, where it can be much easier to paddle downstream than upstream. Sometimes there are rocks and logs just below the surface. Notice how the water makes small **riffles** or waves around them--a good sign to avoid these obstructions. If water is very shallow, the surface above has small waves. The deepest water is marked with a **long V** of smooth water outlined with riffles, as the sketch above shows. If you head for the point of the V you will find the deepest and safest route. A light canoe does not need much water to float. In low water, even with a light canoe, you may have to get out and walk your boat through the shallowest stretches. If the water ahead appears very rough, get out and examine it carefully from shore. The streams in this chapter are generally safe for flatwater canoeing, but high water from lots of rain can change that.

Trees often fall across streams. You can carry over them in the same way you carry over beaver dams. However, if there is any current, it may push your canoe into the fallen logs. In heavy current these logs can be dangerous, and canoeists refer to them as **sweepers** or **strainers**.

Most of these streams still have sluggish places, filled with reeds and grasses, where there is almost no current. You still have to be alert to the direction of the current to avoid side channels. Remember that the direction pointed by underwater vegetation is your best clue.

Adirondack Map--
Longer Trips with One Put-in

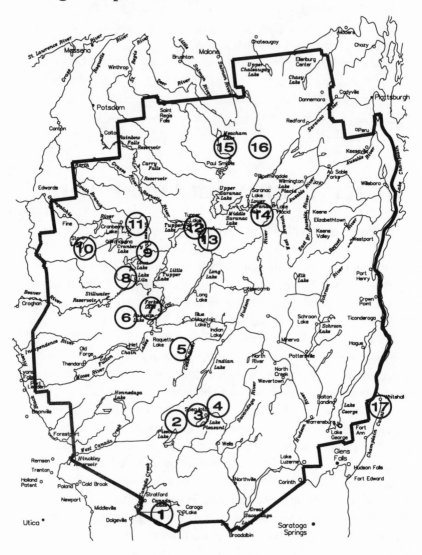

In this chapter, trips in the southern Adirondack are described first, then those in the western, northwestern, and northern Adirondacks. The chapter ends with the one trip from southeastern Adirondack region.

1. Canada Lake Outlet to Stewarts Dam

The round-trip down the outlet of Canada Lake to Stewarts Dam is a long day's adventure. The south shores of the outlet are almost all state land. In recent years, numerous summer camps have been built along the northern shores west of Lily Lake.

From the West Lake launch site, paddle down Sawdust Creek to West Lake, south through the channel into Canada Lake and along Dolgeville Point into Lily Lake. The breadth of the lakes here makes it desirable to start the trip on a calm day. Lily Lake marshes are a great place for ducks. At 2 miles, the outlet narrows to form Sprite Creek; watch out for underwater rocks at the outlet of Lily Lake and at the big bend farther downstream. You should not have trouble missing them--steamers used to take passengers all the way to Stewarts Dam at the turn of the last century. There are a few rocks and patches of high ground on the State-owned south shore for picnicking on the way. In summer, there is little current and often a prevailing west wind in the afternoon to speed your return.

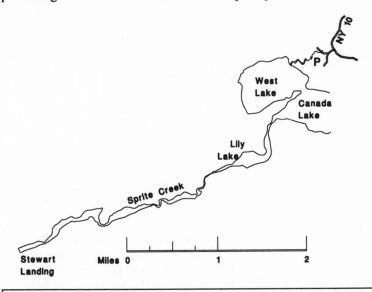

Distance - 10 miles round-trip
Time - 5 hours
Launch - DEC's West Lake Fishing Access site, see page 59.

71

2. Fall Stream

The beginning of Fall Stream is sluggish and deep and can be canoed in low summer water. It is easy to paddle the 1.7 miles upstream to Fall Lake; it helps if beaver have dammed the stream farther north, for then there is surely enough water behind their dams to float you into Vly Lake, 4.5 miles from the road. You meet small riffles in the shallows at least two points, more if the beaver have not done their work. A picnic rock slopes steeply to the water on the east shore about 0.4 mile across Vly Lake.

On rare occasions you can continue through the inlet stream in the northwest corner of that lake all the way to Mud Pond providing the beaver have dammed the stream to make it deep enough for canoeing.

Cardinal flower

Distance - 10 miles round-trip
Time - 5 hours
Launch site - To begin the trip, drive west from NY 8 on Old Piseco Road, headed toward the airport. At 1.6 miles, you cross Fall Stream and just beyond, on the north side of the road, there is a short roadway that leads to the flatwater portion of the stream. This access is privately owned, permission from the Irondequoit Club to use it may be required. No camping, fires, or picnicking are permitted here and it is best to park back close to Old Piseco Road in a way that does not block access.

3. Moffit Beach, Sacandaga Lake, to Mud Pond

The short stretch of Burnt Place Brook that connects Sacandaga Lake to Mud Pond is a most inviting canoe stream. However, to reach it, you have to canoe 1.2 miles west across Sacandaga Lake from the boat launch at Moffit Beach Campground, something that should only be tried on a calm day. Then you head north for a mile to find Burnt Place Brook where it empties into the very northernmost lobe of Sacandaga Lake. Follow the brook due north through as it winds through a broad marsh for 0.8 mile, then narrows for another 0.5 mile before entering 0.3-mile-long Mud Pond. It is possible to continue canoeing for 0.3 mile north on the inlet of Mud Pond.

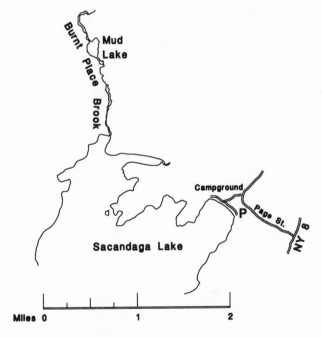

Distance - 7.6 miles round-trip
Time - 4 to 5 hours
Launch - Turn north from NY 8 on Campground Road, 1.6 miles southwest of Speculator. Signs point to Moffit Beach Campground; there is a day-use fee.

4. Kunjamuk River

The Kunjamuk River leads north into International Paper Company's Speculator Tree Farm. You can head upriver as far as you would like as long as you can return the same day; there is no camping on the tract. It is certainly possible to canoe up to Elm Lake and back in a day, although your trip may be slowed because the Kunjamuk is occasionally dammed by beaver or blocked by fallen trees.

Paddle down river on the Main Branch of the Sacandaga, which is the outlet of Lake Pleasant. The Kunjamuk flows into the Sacandaga in the midst of a large marsh filled with pickerelweed, 1.5 miles from the put-in. Turn north just before the houses and rapids on the Main Branch. The Kunjamuk winds north for 1.8 miles to the valley between Rift and Cave hills. To the east, 0.4 mile, into the valley lies Kunjamuk Cave, a small sinkhole opening.

You pass a sand pit in another 0.8 mile, So far the twists and turns of the river make it seem much longer. In another mile, you enter Elm Lake, which extends 0.7 mile to the north. You can paddle north of Elm Lake, but it is about a six-hour round-trip to the lake, so watch the time.

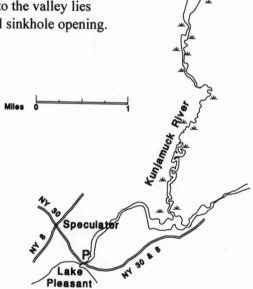

Distance - 12 miles round-trip
Time - 6 or more hours
Launch site - Park to the west of NY 30 in the town field south of Speculator, just beyond the pavilion. Launch in the river nearby.

Several species of alders line the swamps beside many Adirondack streams.

5. Cedar River Flow

Cedar River Flow is a nearly 3-mile long body of water held back by Wakely Dam. Paddling the Cedar River Flow south to the reed beds at the end of the flow is easy if you are not facing a headwind. Finding the channel in the reeds that will take you on upstream is not easy. At its confluence with the flow, the Cedar River has almost no perceptible current. There are many different blind channels leading into the marsh and even the correct channel has many side waterways that can confuse you.

Paddle south for about 3 miles along the eastern shore of the flow, past several spruce- and balsam-covered knolls with marshes between. The reed beds begin about halfway to the southern end, but if you stick fairly close to the eastern shore you should find the river channel, which enters the flow in the southeast corner of the flow. Grass pointing downstream may be your only indication that you are in a flowing stream.

Beyond the weed beds, the sluggish river winds upstream through the marsh and past two steep banks for 1.5 miles to a lean-to. You can continue up the Cedar River for another 0.5 mile to a gravelly, shallow, swift-moving section of river.

If you can paddle or push your canoe above this, there is still another mile of flatwater to enjoy on the Cedar River.

to
Indian Lake
and NY 28

Wakely
Dam

Cedar

River

Flow

Miles 0 1

Many species of ferns grow at streamside.

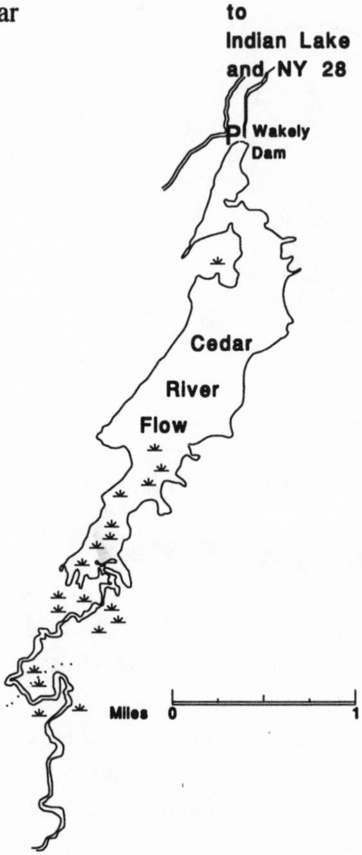

Distance - 12 miles
Time - A full day if you have to search about for the proper channel.
Launch site - To reach Wakely Dam, head west of Indian Lake Village on NY 28. Just past the bridge over the Cedar River, Cedar River Road heads southwest. Follow it 12.3 miles southwest to a large field. The continuing road to the west is the entrance to the Moose River Plains. Camping is permitted in the field. Turn left through it to the beach near the dam where you can launch your canoe.

6. Big Moose Lake to the Eastern Inlets

Like most big lakes, Big Moose can be very rough for paddling. However, the two eastern inlets are so wonderful that they bear waiting for calm enough weather to try these outings. East Bay, the inlet at the southeast corner of the lake, is shorter with a small marsh. A dock on the northern shore gives access to a 1-mile trail that leads to Russian Lake, passing through a beautiful old-growth forest on the way.

Northeast Inlet is a 1.2-miles-long, broad expanse of water bordered by marshes. Osprey nest in one of the tall dead trees near the water. Pickerelweeds color the waterway; great blue heron, kingfishers, and many birds abound. The channel narrows and splits near its eastern end. One channel ends at the beginning of the 0.5 mile trail to the lean-to at Andys Creek.

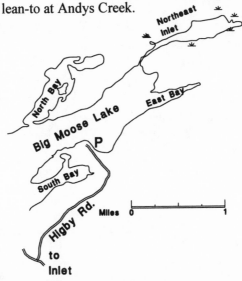

Distance - 2.8 miles round-trip to the end of East Bay, 5 miles round-trip to the end of Northeast Inlet, 6 miles approximately for a circuit of both inlets.

Time - 4 hours or more to explore Northeast Inlet.

Launch - From the Big Moose Association launch site. Drive 3.9 miles north of NY 28 at Inlet on Big Moose Road, turn right onto Higby Road for 1.5 miles and bear right to the dock. Park so as not to block residents' cars.

7. Forked Lake and Brandreth Lake Outlet

Brandreth Lake Outlet flows into the long western arm of Forked Lake. Only the far western end of Forked Lake and the eastern shores near Forked Lake Campground are state owned. From the launch at the carry between Raquette and Forked Lakes, paddle 1.4 miles west on Forked Lake to the marshes at the western end. Brandreth Lake Outlet is broad and marshy where it enters Forked Lake. Great blue heron often stand watchfully in the shallows. As the stream narrows, it is apt to be blocked by beaver dams. There is a small rapids with a short, wet trail to the left where you can carry around the rapids. The stream become narrower and narrower, the current a little stronger, so that it is not easy to reach the boundary of private land 1.5 miles from the lake, where you have to turn around.

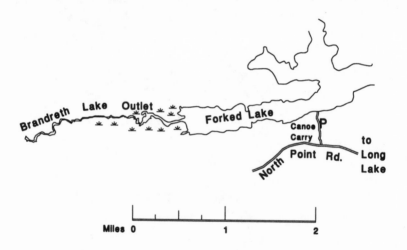

Distance - 6 miles
Time - half-day
Launch - At the north end of the carry between Raquette and Forked lakes. The marked carry is the dirt road to the right from North Point Road, 9.1 miles from Deerland, and a little past the bridge over the Raquette River. See also directions to Forked Lake Campground, page 34, which forks right from North Point Road. The carry is over private land; park in the designated area and observe all signs.

8. Lake Lila

More than a century ago, Dr. William Seward Webb bought large tracts in the northwestern Adirondacks mostly in the Beaver River watershed. He built the railroad that connected the Mohawk River with Malone; it became the Adirondack Division of the New York Central Railroad. The center of his holdings became his private estate, which he named Nehasane Park. It surrounded beautiful Smith's Lake, which he renamed Lake Lila, after his wife. All the land is now owned by the state and Lake Lila is the largest lake in the Adirondacks entirely surrounded by state land.

Lake Lila is 2.5 miles long; its deep southern lobe makes it almost that broad. With shores lined with windswept pines, islands, and a huge marsh bay to the south, Lake Lila invites exploring by canoe. No motorboats are allowed, but the size of the lake means winds can make canoeing difficult.

Fifteen designated campsites line the shores, four of them are on islands. You can explore the outlet, the Beaver River, for less than a mile or one inlet, Shingle Shanty Brook, for 1.5 miles, where it winds through marshes before flowing into the southeastern corner of the southern bay.

Distance - 14 miles to explore the lake and its inlet and outlet.
Time - at least a day
Launch - Launch at the end of a 0.3 mile carry-trail that leads south from the parking area. Turn west from NY 30, 7 miles north of Long Lake to County Route 10 A, or west on County Route 10, south of Tupper Lake. Routes 10 and 10 A intersect near Little Tupper Lake (private land) and continue west as Sabattis Road for 4.6 miles to a left fork, which is Lake Lila access road. The parking area is 5.8 miles down this dirt road; parking is limited and there is no parking along the access road.

9. Bog River to Hitchins Pond

Around the turn of the century, Augustus A. Low, a wealthy China trader from New York City, purchased a large tract of land surrounding the headwaters of the Bog River. He had dams built on the river, which was then a dismal chain of bogs and ponds. The lower dam created a stretch of flatwater through the bogs; the upper dam created a beautiful long lake, best enjoyed by canoe camping.

The first part of the river is bordered by rock walls topped by tall pines, and at 1 mile the route swings right into a boggy lowland. The river bends left at 1.3 miles so you can now see the Adirondack Railroad tracks ahead. You go under the railroad at 1.6 miles. The route winds through more boggy lowlands lined with tamarack and pine, and enters Hitchins Pond at 2.5 miles. You can explore the eastern lobe of the pond to your right; it is 0.5 mile long. At the head of the lobe to the left, 0.65 miles away, is Low's Upper Dam and the carry for Lows Lake. No motorboats are allowed on Hitchins Pond and wildlife abounds.

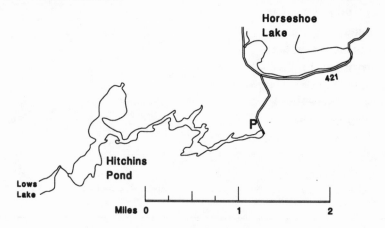

Distance - 7.3 or more miles, round-trip, with exploring Hitchins Pond.
Time - 3 hours
Launch - Turn west on NY 421 from NY 30, at the south end of Tupper Lake, and continue for 5.9 miles to a left turn near the southwest corner of Horseshoe Lake. You reach the Lower Dam in another 0.8 miles on the left fork. Launch just upstream from the dam.

10. Little River

The Little River was originally called the Little Oswegatchie for the larger river into which it flows. It *is* a very little river, even though it traces a long, winding route through flatlands west of Cranberry Lake. The river is dark, stained with mud and vegetable matter, so it is hard to see rocks or logs beneath the surface. But, it has very pretty marshy shores, a winding course, and more than a few beaver dams and obstructions.

From the put-in, paddle south, upstream through marshes bright in fall with asters and Joe-Pye weed. Tall black cherry trees rise above the edges of the marsh. The river twists, then follows two straight sections before picking up Mud Creek at 1.5 miles and making a hairpin bend to the northeast. The marshes continue for 0.6 mile more until surrounding mountains draw close beside the river. You have to carry over logs across the river as well as beaver dams. The river

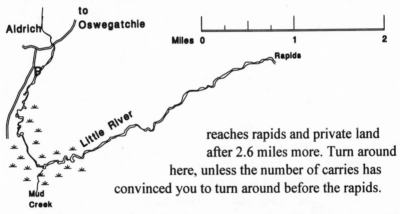

reaches rapids and private land after 2.6 miles more. Turn around here, unless the number of carries has convinced you to turn around before the rapids.

Distance - 9.4 miles round-trip
Time - 5 hours or more depending on the number of carries
Launch - Turn south from NY 3 toward Oswegatchie. Turn left at the first intersection, then right at about 1 mile (before you cross the railroad tracks) on Coffin Mills Road. Pass Coffin Mills at 2.2 miles and Aldrich at 4 miles. Turn left past the barrier into Aldrich Pond Wild Forest at 4.3 miles and park at about 4.6 miles near designated campsite 1. The shortest path to the river and the first one above the rapids starts from that campsite. You will recognize the put-in on the return by the big iron ring in the large boulder at water's edge--the ring once held a boom to contain logs floated down the river.

11. Massawepie Mire on the Grass River

The Grass does grow wide enough to justify the name river, but its headwaters are very small. Its twists and turns are so tight that it is almost impossible to measure them, even on the new large-scale maps! This trip takes you downstream at first. There is a slight current in low water, just enough to make you cautious about how far you paddle before turning around.

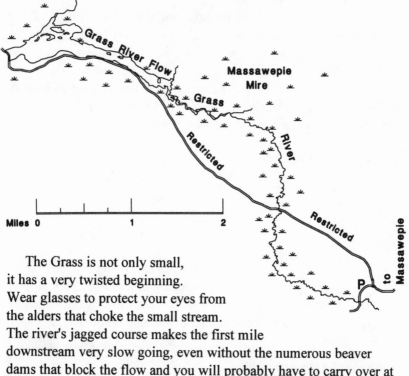

The Grass is not only small, it has a very twisted beginning. Wear glasses to protect your eyes from the alders that choke the small stream. The river's jagged course makes the first mile downstream very slow going, even without the numerous beaver dams that block the flow and you will probably have to carry over at least a half dozen of them. The river is a bit wider and straighter after it passes the Grass River Club buildings, heavily posted inholdings (private tracts surrounded by state land) in the midst of the easement lands that permit access to the river. At 2.5 miles, you paddle under a bridge that carried the old Emporium Railroad.

The railroad bed is now owned by the Nature Conservancy so that it is possible to reach this point by carrying your canoe (driving is not permitted) along the railroad bed from the access road. This will eliminate the twistiest part of the trip, but the length of the carry, more than a mile, means that you would need a wheeled cart.

The river as far as the railroad crossing is bordered with a dull mix of reeds, grasses, and alders. The widening river improves views of pines and tamaracks that crown the low eskers that edge the swamp containing the river. (Eskers are ridges of sand that were deposited by rivers flowing under glaciers.) The swamp is the huge Massawepie Mire, which covers many square miles east of Tupper Lake. You ⓪ reach Burnt Rock, a 40-foot promontory, at 3.7 miles. It takes long **WEST** enough, two and a half to three hours, to reach this point that you may want to turn around here.

Beyond, the river swings west, picks up the outlet of Massawepie Lake, and after 2 miles flows into 2-mile long Grass River Flow, which was originally dammed for logging. It is filled with stumps, beaver dams, and sometimes confusing channels. Private land blocks access at the end of the flow and the river beyond is full of rapids, so you have to turn around here. On the way back, the twists and turns all look remarkably similar. Where the channel splits you are apt to pick the wrong channel a few times, unless you watch carefully for signs of flow. Allow extra time for searching about.

Access is through the Massawepie Scout Reservation, which is open to the public from September 1 through June 15. There is no access on the easement lands surrounding the river between hunting season and December 31. That means canoeing is pretty much limited to September or bug season in spring.

Distance - up to 15 miles round-trip
Time - Figure as much as 50 minutes a mile for the first part of the trip.
Launch site - Massawepie Scout Reservation is 5.3 miles west of Piercefield on NY 3. Drive south and stop at 0.3 mile where registration is required. Pick up a sketch map that shows where you can park to canoe the reservation's lakes and ponds in the off-season. Continue past Catamount Pond, Massawepie Pond, Horseshoe, Deer and Town Line ponds to an intersection at 4.3 miles. (Part of the road is carved out of the side of the tall esker that separates the ponds.) Continue to a four-way intersection at 4.6 miles and turn right. In 0.2 mile, turn left, and at 5.1 miles you reach a parking area that is 100 yards short of the bridge over the Grass. Put-in beside the bridge on the north side.

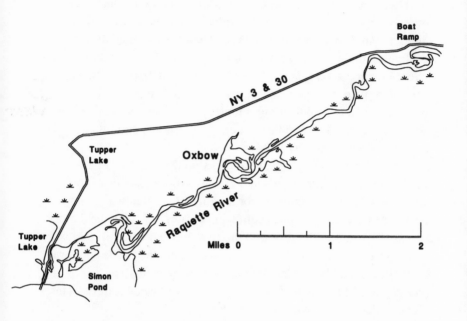

12. Raquette River

The Raquette River is one of the Adirondack's most picturesque waterways. Motorboat use is heavy, but that should not deter the canoeist, especially if there is a mid-week time when traffic on the river is light.

Canoe west, downriver, to the marshes bordering Simon Pond. The 4-miles as-the-crow-flies stretches to many more as the river winds and twists about through its broad flooded course. At about the halfway point, you can explore an oxbow that winds north of the river in a complete circle.

Canoe east, upstream toward Axton, a second launch site 13 miles southeast. In several places, you are sure to be tricked into taking the wrong channel because the current is so slow. One channel that leads south to private land and Follensby Pond is blocked to canoes at present.

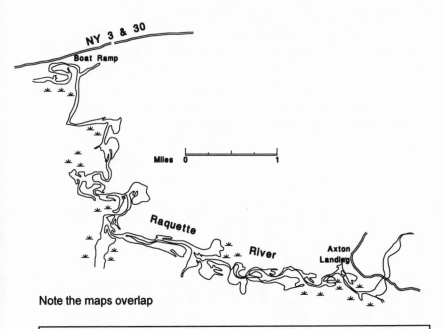

Note the maps overlap

Distance - 14 miles round-trip to Simon Pond; 14 miles round-trip west to Axton Landing.
Time - A full day in either direction.
Launch site - The DEC launch site and parking area, 1.6 miles west of the intersection of NY 3 and 30 in Wawbeek, and east of Tupper Lake.

13. Raquette River, Axton to High Falls

The round-trip up the Raquette River from Axton to High Falls and back is a great one-day canoe trip into the wilderness, that is if you are prepared to see motorboats and hoards of canoe campers. The paddle south is along a wide river, posted on the west side. Numerous bays and blind channels branch from the river which has so little current that you may occasionally take a wrong turn.

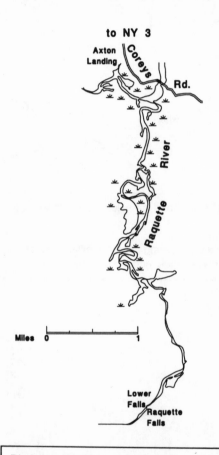

Flatwater ends near a big field on the east side of the river just below rapids. A trail, also on the east side, leads up along the falls. A walk to the falls, which actually is a series of falls, takes an hour or so.

Paul Jamieson's *Canoe Routes - North Flow* (Adirondack Mountain Club) not only describes the route in greater detail, but it entertains with some of the river's history.

Distance - 12 miles, round-trip
Time - a full day
Launch - Axton Landing: Drive west of the intersection of NY 3 and 30 at Wawbeek Corners for almost 3 miles to Coreys Road. Turn right, south on Coreys Road for 3 miles to the landing.

14. Chubb River

The Chubb River is a very small stream that arises on the western slopes of Street and Nye mountains, two of the Adirondack High Peaks, and flows north toward Lake Placid. A 4.2-mile stretch in the valley south of Averyville Road winds quietly at first through a wild marshy stretch bordered with cedars. Dark conifers line the steeper banks and a mile from the start, there is a 0.25-mile carry around rapids. Where the river is wide, there is little current; where it narrows you have to work to paddle upstream.

Farther south, marshes again border the river, their broad expanse providing views of Street and Nye and the slides that scar the mountain's northwestern slopes. Beaver dams occur in various places depending on the food supply--alders, swamp maples, popple, and even cedar. The dams slow the dark brown water as well as your trip upstream. Count the species of birds on the trip, and you will be surprised at the number you will find. Others have reported seeing osprey, ravens, black-backed three-toed woodpeckers, herons and many ducks. When the river becomes too narrow and the current too strong, turn around and enjoy the wild scenery all over again.

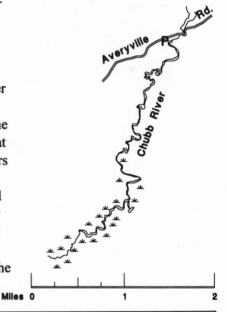

Miles 0   1   2

Distance - 8.4 miles, round-trip
Time - A full day's outing
Launch - Old Military Road bypasses Lake Placid on the south, connecting NY 86 with NY 73. About halfway between those connections, Averyville Road heads southwest. Follow Averyville Road to the bridge over the Chubb River. Just beyond is a marked parking area for the Northville-Placid Trail. The launch site at the lower end of the first beaver flow can be found at the end of a short path that starts across the road from the parking area.

15. Osgood River

The Osgood River is very short (about 15 miles from the outlet of Osgood Pond to Meacham Lake), very narrow, and rocky beyond the dam on the outlet of Osgood Pond. In the north, just south of Meacham Lake, the river winds and twists sluggishly through marshes bordered on the east by eskers. There is a range of small mountains beyond.

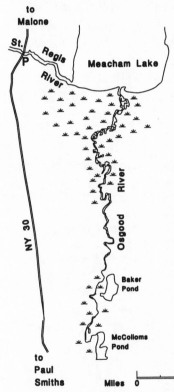

Paddle east from the launch by the bridge on the East Branch of the St. Regis River for 0.6 mile to the lake, then around the southern shore for 0.5 mile to the inlet, the Osgood River.

The Osgood is canoeable for 4 or more twisting miles south of the lake, much of that bordered by state land. At first it winds through broad marshes. Four small bodies of water lie to the east of the river. You can paddle up the short outlets of two of them, Baker and Mud ponds, to visit or camp on their eastern shores. McColloms Pond is hidden from the river by an esker. Climb the southern end of the esker, which is on state land, to look down on the pond. You can spend more than a day paddling south on the river and back.

Distance - 10.2 miles round-trip
Time - At least a full day
Launch - Launch near the bridge over the East Branch of the St. Regis, which is just south of the southern entrance to Meacham Lake Campground. The East Branch of the St. Regis is the outlet of Meacham Lake. You can also launch from the campground, but that adds 2 miles of paddling on open water and a day-use fee.

16. Rainbow and Kushaqua Lakes

Additional Information - *Canoe Routes in Southern Franklin County*, see page 118.

From the bridge over Kushaqua Narrows, paddle south on Rainbow Narrows and west on Rainbow Lake for 2.5 miles to the Inlet Flow, a narrow break in the esker that cuts through the western end of Rainbow Lake. The lake is a long arc, bordered on the south shore with many camps and on the north shore with a wonderful esker topped with pines. When you round the opening into the Flow, you are in another world. From here you can canoe north for about 2 miles, past headlands, dark bays, and more eskers.

The 9-mile circuit can be extended to 11.4 miles by starting at Buck Pond Campground, more if you explore part of Kushaqua Lake.

Distance - 9 or 11.4 miles
Time - 6 hours
Launch - The bridge over Kushaqua Narrows, see page 65-66, or from Buck Pond Campground, page 36.

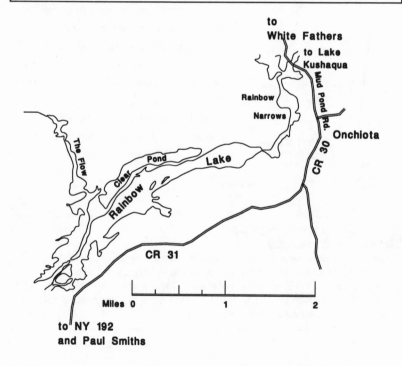

17. South Bay of Lake Champlain

The South Bay of Lake Champlain curves southwest for 3.3 miles from the highway bridge on NY 22, northeast of Whitehall. The north shore is punctuated with marshes and inlets. Tall mountains shelter the bay, whose marshy southern tip offers 2 miles more paddling. This is the really wonderful part of the trip. The south end of the bay is full of pickerelweed and marsh milkweed. The tall cliffs on Diameter loom over the water and offer shelter to nesting hawks. Rattlesnakes inhabit crevices in these rocks.

South of the open water, the stream breaks into narrow channels and smaller bays overshadowed by tall silver maples. It is hard to find the continuing streams, some of which are very shallow. You may explore a few deadends before you find the one that leads to South Bay Brook, but this will give you the opportunity to see many birds. There is a small, dry hummock where you can lunch. Beyond, South Bay Brook narrows between tall banks which are covered in late summer with sweet-smelling blooms. Take a flower book in a sealed plastic bag on this trip. Canoeing ends when the stream is just too small to continue.

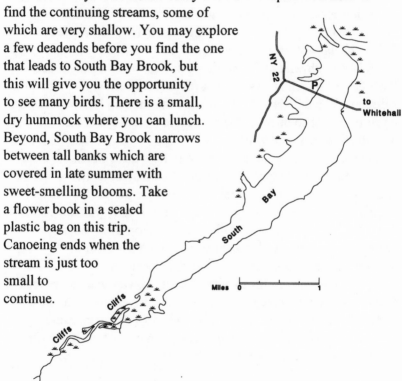

Distance - more than 10 miles, round-trip exploring the narrows
Time - 6 or more hours
Launch - The DEC boat launch site on the north side of NY 22 and on the west side of the bridge over the narrows of Lake Champlain.

Two-Car or Shuttle Routes

When our country was young, water transportation was the only way to travel long distances. Because the rivers in the valleys that surround the central dome of the Adirondacks are all too often wild, tumbling, rocky waterways, the Adirondacks was one of the last places in the country to be settled. These wild rivers are best suited for whitewater canoeing in spring when the water is high. Most of them were once highways for driving logs to mills downstream before the days of trains or trucks.

Valleys with wild or flat stretches of river had the only relatively flat areas for traveling and the first roads were built in them. In the Adirondacks today those first roads are our modern highways, so it is no surprise that so many of the canoeable waterways in the region are near roads, towns, and villages.

On the other hand, quite a few rivers flow through remote areas and it is fortunate that any road reaches them at all to give you access. A canoe trip with a different take-out from the put-in (the end and beginning launch sites), where the current can carry you downstream, can often be one of the great wilderness experiences. The only problem is figuring out a way to drive to both ends and in between--in other words, how to manage the shuttle.

It is best for these trips to have at least two cars and two canoes so one car can be left at the take-out while the drivers return to the put-in. Often the shuttle can add several hours to a day of canoeing.

In this chapter, two canal trips are presented first, then trips in the southern, western, and northern Adirondacks.

Adirondack Map--Two-car or Shuttle Routes

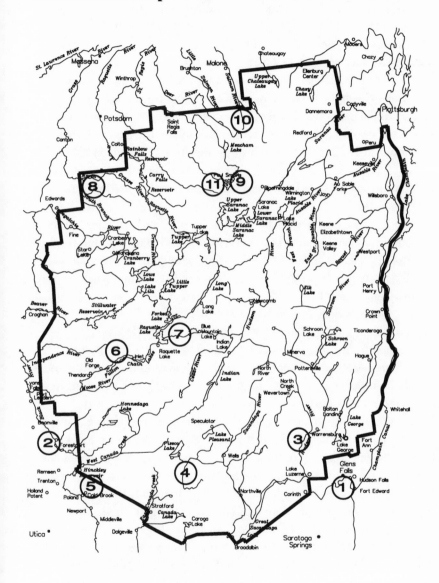

1. Hudson River Feeder Canal

The Feeder Canal just outside the Adirondack Park between Glens Falls and Hudson Falls offers one of the most varied canoe trips anywhere. The Erie Canal from the head of flatwater on the Hudson north of Albany west to the Great Lakes near Niagara Falls was completed in 1825. The Champlain Canal connecting the Hudson with Lake Champlain was completed two years earlier, but the middle of the canal was higher than either of its ends, so additional water was needed. New dams on the Hudson and the Feeder Canal were built in 1822 and 1823 to bring water from the Hudson River above Glens Falls to the Champlain Canal. A series of locks was added to lift canalboats from the Champlain Canal to the level of Hudson Falls.

The Feeder Canal above the locks is the only surviving part of the original Erie Canal system that carries water and boats, though today it is used by canoes instead of the 90-foot-long and 19-foot-wide canalboats that carried logs, lumber, limestone, coal, and paper to factories and markets.

The Feeder Canal still carries water to maintain the level of the modern Champlain Canal. For that reason, a steady flow is maintained from early spring to late fall. The water is usually no more than 2-feet deep. There is a gentle current, and it is possible to paddle both down and upstream, though if a shuttle can be arranged, a through route is best.

The canal starts just below the Feeder Dam on the Hudson. This was the site of the Big Boom that held logs cut in the Adirondacks for sorting and shipping on to the mills. The first part of the canal is lined with the original cut stones, the same kind that were used on the Erie. The canal goes through a lovely forest, then industrial lands and right through the middle of downtown Glens Falls. It flows under a portion of the Finch, Pruyn and Co. paper mill; logs were floated on the canal to this mill until 1946. After the canal passes an old limestone company and a cement plant it returns to residential areas and passes under two bridges. The take-out is a 0.25-mile short of the first lock at a stone amphitheater on Martindale Ave.

The put-in, take-out, and revival of the canal with its hiking paths and picnic parks have been the work of the Feeder Canal Alliance, a group based in Glens Falls (518-792-5363). No other canoe trip can demonstrate as effectively how valuable Adirondack waterways were during the last century.

Distance - 5 miles
Time - 2 to 2 1/2 hours downstream
Put-in - Feeder Dam Park: Exit 18 of the Northway east to first light, right following brown Feeder Canal Park signs.
Take-out - Martindale Park, off Martindale Ave. in Hudson Falls.
Shuttle route - Continue east on Corinth then Broad streets into Glens Falls and head toward Hudson Falls on Warren Street, then turn southeast on NY 32. Turn right and briefly head toward Fort Edward on NY 4 over the canal to Martindale Ave.

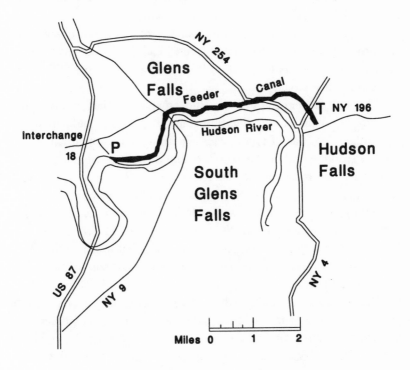

Note change of scale

2. Black River Feeder Canal

The Black River Feeder Canal was built
to carry water from the Black River to the
Erie Canal. Governor DeWitt Clinton knew
as early as 1823 that his "ditch," the Erie
Canal, completed in 1825, would dry up in
summer. However it was not until 1848 that
the feeder was completed from Punkeyville
(Forestport) to Boonville, where the canal
curves south to empty into Lansingkill
Creek. The construction of locks south of
Boonville enabled the canal to carry barges
between the Black and the Erie canals.

The scheme never worked as well as expected because the Black
River--even with the reservoirs that were built on its
headwaters--needed all its summer water to run its downstream mills
and provide transportation on that river. In addition, lumbermen
drained the reservoirs in spring to float their logs to paper mills built
along the Black River.

Although feeder canals on the Hudson and the Black rivers were
built for the same reason, diverting water, they could not be more
dissimilar. The Black River Feeder is nothing but a long ditch,
shallower in the middle than at either end of its canoeable length.
Floodgates divert water from the canal to two streams along the way
so that the level of the water in the canal can be lowered when it is
not being used. It is usually canoeable in summer for its entire length,
but it is wise to check the depth at the crossing of Millers Woods
Road on your way to spotting a car at the take-out in Boonville. At
present there is no monitored phone which you can call to learn about
the water level.

The current is light, even when water is being diverted through the
canal for the Erie. The towpath beside the canal is used by hikers and
bicyclers. You may find a few logs fallen across the canal and maybe
a beaver dam to carry over. The canal is never more than a few feet
deep, placid so that it reflects the sky and overhanging trees, and
quiet, despite the intervening roads.

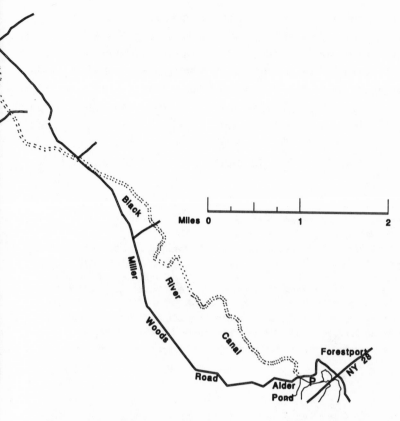

Beyond the put-in at Alder Pond, you pass three small wetlands to the west of the canal. Tall hemlocks and maples give the canal a wild setting. The canal is high above the Black River on the edge of an escarpment here. (An escarpment is a long, steep slope or cliff, bordering a level area.) It is 3.4 miles to the first highway bridge on Edmunds Road. A small footbridge is so low you have to really duck to go under it. At 4.55 miles, you cross under Millers Woods Road, and 0.4 mile beyond is one of the small dams that regulate the side streams. The scenery here is bucolic (typical of rural or farm life), with open fields to the east. At 5.6 miles you cross Lachausse Road and Hays Road East. This is where the canal is the driest--sometimes nothing more than mud flats--so if it is deep enough for canoes here, the entire canal ought to be canoeable.

At 6.4 miles you cross under Hawkinsville Road. A powerline intrudes just beyond. At 8.3 miles you cross under Moose River Road, where a long carry downhill would take you to the beginning of the canoeable stretch of the Black. The canal beyond has begun its wide curve toward Boonville and into the valley of Mill Creek. You can see NY 12 ahead and at 8.7 miles you cross under an iron bridge. A dam that controls the flow of water into Mill Creek follows, then a cross road at 9 miles. The first houses do not interrupt the scenery until you reach 9.4 miles. The trip ends at 9.8 miles, near NY 12 in Boonville.

Distance - 9.8 miles, one way
Time - 5 to 6 hours
Put-in - Turn left from NY 28 just before the bridge over Kayuta Lake. Take the first left in 0.2 mile and follow it for 0.25 mile to the shore of Alder Pond, where there is parking and a good put-in from the causeway.
Take-out - The parking area on the north side of the canal, just across from the Boonville Municipal Park on NY 12.
Shuttle - Follow back roads if you want to check water levels, but the most direct route is down NY 12 and north on NY 28 to Forestport.

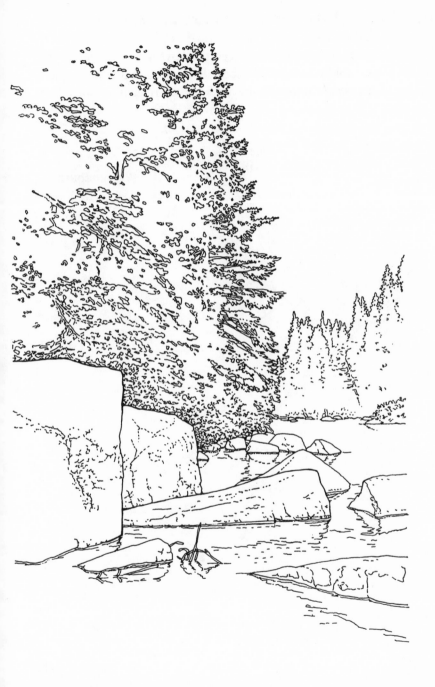

3. Hudson River, Warrensburg to Luzerne

The Hudson River offers a wonderful, long day of canoeing in the southern Adirondacks. In high water, the current is swift and pushes your canoe rapidly along in the northern portion. In low water, there is still a noticeable current in the north but the river is so sluggish in

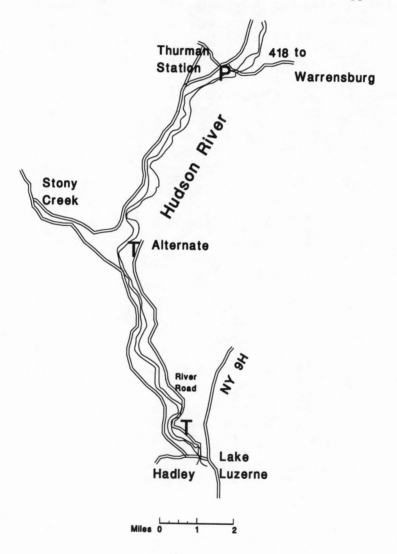

Note change of scale

the south you really have to paddle if there is a headwind. Also, in low water, there are a few places where the river is so shallow over its gravel bottom that you may have to get out and walk your canoe along. The river is bordered on the east by beautiful forests and steep-sloped mountains. There are signs of civilization on the west, but not until you reach the very southern end will you see many buildings.

As soon as you put-in, the current takes you to the far eastern shore and a slight drop shoots your canoe forward. This is the steepest drop in the entire trip. At first you hardly have to paddle, the current is sufficient. The northern portion of the eastern shore is Forest Preserve with a number of picnic spots. You pass a golf course on the right bank, small sharp cliffs drop to the water on the west.

The alternate take-out is at a deep bend, before the confluence with Stony Creek. You encounter rocky flats where Stony Creek flows in from the west. Beyond, the river is broader with several gravel islands.

As the current slows, you will spot several rock landings; if the weather is warm, they are good places to pull up and go for a swim. Field and houses border the lower river, which is very broad. Watch carefully for the cedar tree that marks the take-out!

Distance - 16 miles (8 miles)
Time - 6 hours (3 hours)
Put-in - The parking area west of the bridge over the Hudson at Thurman Station, on Route 418, west of Warrensburg.
Take-out - Beside a parking turnout 0.8 mile north of Luzerne on River Road. Steep chute to water. Note that only a huge cedar tree and no sign marks the take-out spot. Study it carefully so you will not head toward the dangerous falls in Luzerne.
(To shorten the trip, a take-out has been built farther north on River Road. A gate and a sign-in mark the entrance to the park area that is managed by Warren County. North of the gate there is a newly constructed launch with step leading down to it. There is a fee.)
Shuttle - Head south on River Road to the center of Luzerne, turn right toward Hadley, cross the Hudson, and turn right toward Stony Creek. Follow County Route 1 north to Stony Creek, then turn east on Route 418 to the parking area in Thurman.

---

4. West Branch Sacandaga River to Shaker Place

This wonderful one-way trip has a very easy shuttle and can be expanded by adding the one-way trips described on pages 60 and 61. The West Branch rises in the heart of the Silver Lake Wilderness, its three headwater streams joining east of NY 10 to flow north. Because Piseco Lake stretched south through the NY 10 valley during the glacial age, here the river flows through the flat, sandy remnants of the lakebed. Flatwater ends near the sandy fields of Shaker Place,

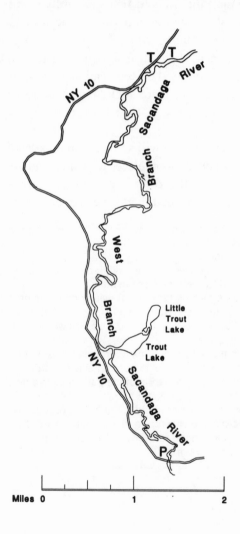

which was once farmed. Below the flatwater section, the river picks up Piseco Outlet, then drops precipitously through some of the wildest gorges and forestland in the Adirondacks.

The flatwater stretch described here is a perfect day's outing, which can be extended with several side trips. The river has everything: remoteness, surrounding small mountains, meanders through marshes and fields of flowers and butterflies. You will always find cardinal flowers in bloom in August.

Canoe downstream from the put-in by the bridge for 2 miles to the entrance to Trout lakes, see page 61, explore them and other channels if you have time. Beyond the entrance to Trout Lake, the river twists and turns through the broad marshes, in two places the oxbows nearly double back on themselves.

In 2.3 miles more, you reach a point below Avery's, the big hotel on NY 10. Beyond the marshes below Avery's, the river moves away from the highway to flow east of Pine Mountain. In another mile you reach an old bridge for a logging road. You may have to carry over its remains. Two more streams, the outlets of the Loomis Ponds, flow in also on the right. When the river emerges into marshes again, the road is not far from away, nor is the end of the trip.

Even though the route is all downstream, the current is so mild it does not compensate for any headwind you might encounter. There are only one or two places where the river swings close to wooded and dry shores where you can picnic. One is north of the entrance to Trout Lake, another is opposite the northern slopes of Pine Mountain.

Distance - 8.6 miles, without exploring side channels
Time - 4 to 5 hours
Put-in - The second bridge, 6 miles north of Pine Lake on NY 10, see page 60.
Take-out - Near Shaker Place on NY 10, 6.5 miles north of the second bridge a dirt road forks right and downhill. The road leads close to the river at the end of the flatwater section. If the dirt road appears too wet to drive (it can be, so check), park on the widened part of the highway just south of the road. Here the carry out is short, but very steep.
Shuttle - 6.5 miles along NY 10.

5. Black Creek

Black Creek in the southwestern corner of the Park is a shallow stream, so shallow that your canoe will certainly scrape the rocky bottom in low water. In fact, you may have to get out and walk your canoe along in two or three spots. Nevertheless, it offers a very pleasant and remarkably wild adventure.

From the put-in, paddle upstream for 2.5 miles to an iron bridge on the Gray-Wilmurt Road. This could be an alternate put-in, but it is not recommended because the current is strong just downstream from the bridge. The winding course has overhanging trees, colorful shrubs and plants, and ducks galore. The wetlands in the muddy flats here are especially rich, handsome enough to justify paddling both ways along the creek here. Because of the current, it takes an hour and a quarter to paddle upstream, 50 minutes to return to the bridge at NY 8. This is the wildest part of the trip and should be enjoyed leisurely.

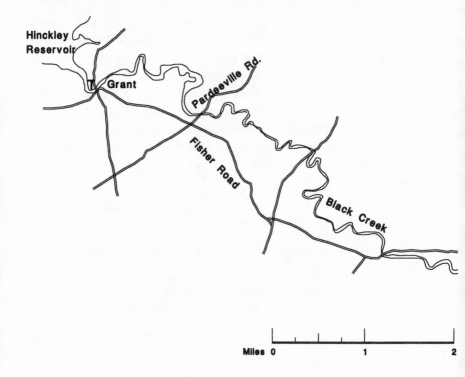

Downstream from NY 8, it is 1.4 miles to the next bridge (Fisher Road Bridge), but the river changes. The shores are steeper and covered with dense forest. In the next 2.5 mile section to an old bridge abutment, the river winds and twists beneath the dark canopy. It is 1.9 miles to the next bridge at Pardeeville Road, 2.4 miles for the last stretch to Grant. That last section is very broad and open. The river is so quiet and sluggish, it hardly seems to move at all. Signs of civilization and the last bridge alert you to the take-out.

Distance - 13.2 miles
Time - 5 hours
Put-in - The NY 8 bridge crosses over Black Creek about 7.5 miles northeast of Poland or just south of Fisher Road crossing. Here there is a large gravel parking area on the side of NY 8. The put-in is down a steep bank from the parking area.
Take-out - Beside a hotel (ask permission to park there) in Grant, which is where Black Creek empties into Hinckley Reservoir. Check for very low water in the reservoir; this means the creek may be too low for canoeing. Take NY 8 east from Poland to Cold Brook and follow the signs north to Grant, or take NY 365 to Hinckley Road and wind along the south shore of the reservoir to Grant.
Shuttle - From the hotel, cross Black Creek and take the first left, Pardeeville Road, which leads to Fisher Road. Turn south on NY 8.

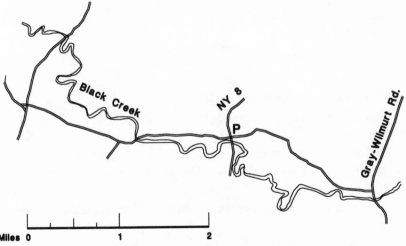

Note that the map repeats

105

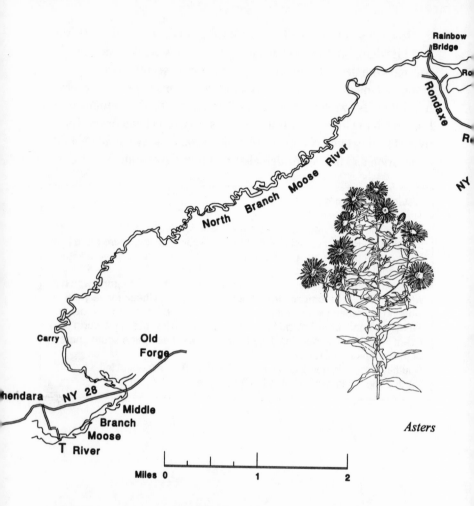

Asters

Miles 0   1   2

6. North Branch Moose River

The entire canoe trip on the North Branch of the Moose is bordered by private lands. The trip is very popular, so pick an off-peak time for it. It is possible arrange help with the shuttle by contacting Moose River Outfitters, see page 29, in advance. It may be only 7 miles "as the crow flies" from the put-in at Rainbow Bridge to the take-out in Thendara, but the paddling distance is almost double that.

The route is generally southwest, but the stream's meanders will take you in every direction of the compass. At first, a gentle current sweeps you along below Rainbow Bridge through countless oxbows. Within a mile, you pass under an iron bridge. The shallow, sandy-based river gradually deepens and becomes more sluggish. Even with a map it is hard to identify landmarks such as the surrounding hills.

Sometimes the stream has a canopy of trees dotted with dark evergreens, sometimes it winds through open marshes. Several sandy beaches make good places to stop for picnics. At several points in the marshes, the stream splits. Sometimes you can try either way, sometimes you have to be careful to identify the current so you won't get sidetracked in a backwater. At 5.5 miles you pass a bridge, then at 7.5 miles, well past the halfway point, you can spot the raised bed of the Adirondack Railroad.

Nearly four hours from the start you will see a warning sign -- danger ahead. You must use the carry here at almost 10 miles, for the river is blocked by a jumble of boulders. The sign marks an easy place to pull your canoe out on the left, east, side of the river. A marked trail, less than 0.2-mile long, leads across a bridge over the river and down to the foot of the rapids. The trail is in the woods almost hidden from the adjacent golf-course.

Once back in the river, you find it widens as it picks up the Middle Branch, which is the outlet of the Fulton Chain of Lakes. Continue downstream on the Middle Branch, under NY 28 at 11.5 miles, then on to the take-out.

Time - 5 to 6 hours
Distance - With twists and turns and oxbows, about 13 miles
Put-in - Turn north on Rondaxe Road from NY 28, 5.1 miles west of the bridge over the Moose west of Old Forge. Stay left past both roads that fork right toward the shores of Rondaxe Lake, then stay right where the road to Adirondack Woodcraft Camp forks left, 1.8 miles from NY 28. The road reaches private land at Rainbow Bridge in another 0.4 mile. The put-in is beside Rainbow Bridge.
Take-out - Thendara, 0.4 mile south of NY 28 on Beech Street, same as for Middle Branch Moose, page 64.
Shuttle - Drive east on NY 28 from Beech Street, cross bridge over the Moose (0 mile), and follow directions to the put-in.

7. Raquette Lake to Blue Mountain Lake,

One of the most popular canoe trips in the Adirondack Park has a long history as a waterway. A visit to the Adirondack Museum will give the details. In 1892, an extension of the Adirondack Railroad was completed from Carter Station to Raquette Lake. There, steamers took passengers across the lake and up the Marion River where the Marion River Railroad carried passengers and baggage on the short trip to Utowana Lake. Today, part of the roadbed for that railroad is the level route of the carry between the two navigable stretches of this trip. Steamers then took passengers from the foot of Utowana Lake to the hotels at Blue Mountain Lake.

From the town beach at Raquette Lake, head northeast, past Big Island to round the north shore of Long Point at 1.5 miles. The bay north of Long point narrows to the outlet of the Marion River in another 1.2 miles. The next 3.8 miles along that river beside its marshes is the best part of the entire canoe trip. The Marion River gradually gets narrower and shallower. At about 6.5 miles, you approach a blind channel. Turn north, left, through a very narrow channel that makes you wonder if you have chosen the right way. The channel curves around south again and reaches a take-out beside railroad bed. Here a 0.5-mile, easy carry leads to a launch at the west end of Utowana Lake.

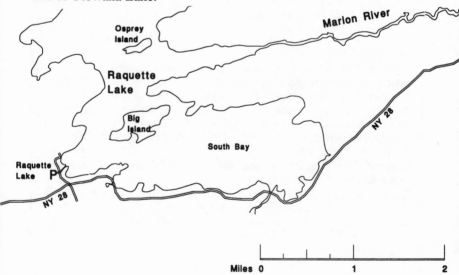

From here on the waterway is broad and open, your paddling usually assisted by the prevailing west winds. Utowana Lake is long (2.6 miles) and thin; it narrows past big rocks near the inlet for 0.5 mile, then opens out again into 1-mile long Eagle Lake. There is a handsome rustic bridge over the inlet of Eagle Lake and another short section of narrow channel before your route opens to the broad expanse of Blue Mountain Lake. Head for the beach in the southeastern lobe of the lake, 2 miles away, 5.1 miles from the carry.

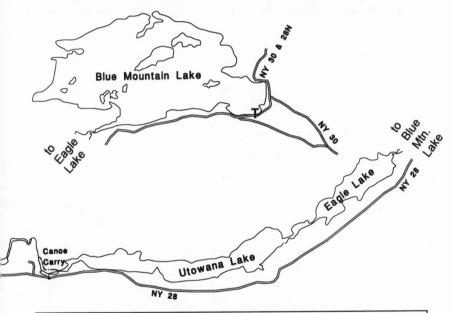

Distance - 13.5 miles, 6.5 from Raquette Lake to the outlet of Utowana Lake, 7 miles from the outlet of Utowana Lake to the beach at Blue Mountain Lake. 0.5 mile of that distance is the carry.

Time - 6 hours

Put-in - The town beach in the hamlet of Raquette Lake, 0.5 mile north of NY 28.

Take-out - The beach at NY 28, 0.5 mile west of the intersection of NY 30 and 28 in Blue Mountain Lake.

Shuttle - Drive west on NY 28 to Raquette Lake. [An alternate launch, which can be used for either half of the trip is from NY 28, 6.3 miles west of Blue Mountain Lake. Look for a path (*not* the nearby dirt road, which is posted) where the highway swings close to shore. Carry along it for 100 yards to the shore near the outlet of Utowana Lake.]

8. Grass River

The Grass River in the northwestern Adirondacks offers a short flatwater stretch between wonderful sections of rapids, flumes, and waterfalls. A new put-in on the Middle Branch of the Grass makes starting the trip easier than ever before. The river is flat enough that you may want to explore it all from that put-in.

From the put-in, paddle downstream for 0.6 mile on the Middle Branch to its confluence with the main river in a wide floodplain lined with silver maples. The old put-in is upstream on the main river

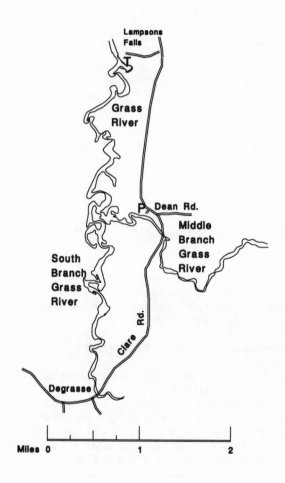

in a State Forest Area just outside the Park. Both the stretch on the Middle Branch and the section upstream on the main river are quiet and remote, good places to see beavers and birds.

Sandy slopes of eskers border the river upstream from the confluence. Paddle this 2.6 miles and return to continue downstream on the Grass River. The last 3.2-mile section between the confluence of the two branches and the take-out above the falls goes all too quickly. Listen for the falls and watch for the foundations of an old powerhouse on the right bank to find the take-out. There are no signs of warning, so be alert to the approach to the falls.

Distance - 9 miles as described
Time - 4 to 5 hours
Put-in - Drive north of Degrasse, (which is north of Fine) on Clare Road or County Route 27. Parking is 0.3 mile north of Clare Road intersection with Dean Road. The put-in is 300 feet away down a path marked with yellow canoe-carry signs.
Take-out - Continue north on Dean Road for about 2.5 miles to a dirt road to the left. Lampson Falls is 0.3 mile west on the dirt road. A path, a short carry, from the road leads to the take-out, just upstream from the falls.
Shuttle - Clare Road and the dirt roads as described.

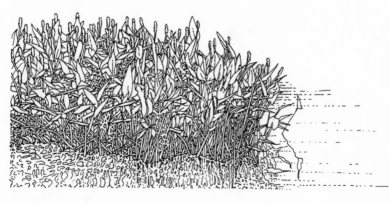

Pickerelweed

9. Jones, Osgood, and Church Ponds

The channel between Jones and Osgood ponds is so shallow you may have to push your canoe through the muddy-bottomed shallows. Osgood has no public launch, so starting at Jones or Church is the only way to enjoy that pond. *INCORRECT- WHITE PINE RD. ACCESS*

Paddle less than 0.5 mile to the outlet in the marsh at the western edge of Jones Pond and less than the access road. Stop along the outlet to enjoy the birds and the esker that borders the 1.6-mile outlet. You cross under an access road 0.3 mile before you enter Osgood Pond. Head northwest through Osgood Pond for a mile until the outlet bay narrows into the Osgood River, which is a flatwater stream for the next 2.5 miles.

The river is broad for the first 2 miles, then narrows, bends west, and ends at a dam. Through most of the way, the river flows through a spruce and tamarack swamp. Sphagnum mats host bog plants along the western shore.

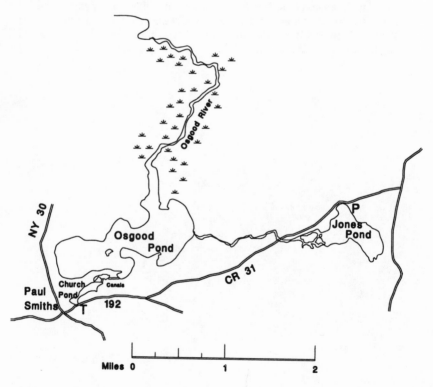

112

Turn around at the dam, and when you are back in the main lake, head west-southwest. A long peninsula separates the pond into two lobes. Head for the southern shore to find a narrow, man-made canal. This dark and mysterious waterway, the most interesting part of the canoe trip, leads past a church, St. John's of the Wilderness, and into Church Pond. Cross the pond to the south to the take-out. It is a mile across Osgood Pond to the canal, 0.7 mile though it and Little Osgood Pond to the take-out on Church Pond.

Distance - 12 miles
Time - 6 hours
Put-in - Drive east of Paul Smiths on NY 192 for 1.2 miles and turn left on County Route 31 in Brighton. In less than 2 miles more cross over the outlet of Jones Pond and continue around the north shore to parking near the marked carry to Rainbow Lake. Put-in from the parking area.
Take-out - On the southern shore of Church Pond, 0.15 mile east of Paul Smiths on NY 192.
Shuttle - Return following the directions for the put-in.

10. Hatch Brook to Salmon River

Hatch Brook is a small, winding brook that flows north into the Salmon River. The Salmon continues to wind, twist, and turn and then, after Big Bend, it flows wide and straight to a take-out just above Chasm Falls.

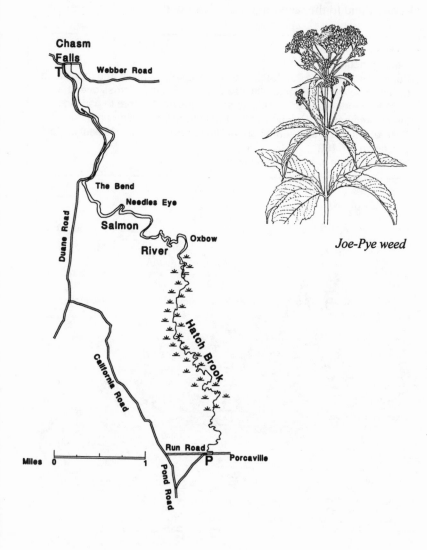

Joe-Pye weed

A fair current, even in low water, sweeps you along the narrow Hatch Brook. You do not have to paddle very much except to steer, and you do a lot of that in the river's tight twists and loops. The alders on the banks really close in on your canoe. Steering through the sharp turns puts your paddling partnership to the test--it is good practice for later on when you want to learn how to canoe on whitewater.

At first, houses border the east side of the brook. Then, past a wild section, the marsh opens up to fields of Joe-Pye weed, and you reach the confluence of Hatch Brook with Salmon River at 3.3 miles. The Salmon is broader and slower moving. Its banks are brightened with cranberry viburnum and elderberries. It is open enough that you have views of Titusville Mountain with its double summit and cliff faces. You finally reach a straight stretch, then after a long gentle curve, you enter, the "eye of the needle"--an oxbow that earned its name because it is so sharp. The end of the oxbow, at 5.6 miles, is tight against a very steep hill. Just beyond, Duane Creek joins the river, then, at 6.2 miles, the river turns sharply north at Big Bend. For the last 1.8 miles, the river is broad and flat, nestled in the deep valley beside Duane Road.

Distance - 8 miles

Time - 4 hours or less

Put-in - On the northwest side of the bridge at Porcaville. Turn east from NY 30, nearly 17 miles north of Paul Smiths, onto Route 99 heading through Duane Corners. When Route 99 forks right, continue straight on County Route 27 (Pond Road). The bridge is 7.3 miles from NY 30. Put-in on the north side of the road, west of the bridge.

Take-out - The west side of the river before the bridge, at the intersection of Duane Road and County Routes 41 and 25.

Shuttle - Go straight west from the Porcaville bridge (Route 27 forks left) onto a narrow dirt track in a pine plantation. Turn right at a T, 0.5 mile from the bridge, onto California Road. Turn right at 2.2 miles, at the next T, heading north on Duane Road. (There is a parking turnout and picnic site at 4.8 miles, which can be used to shorten the trip.) The take-out is at 5.5 miles.

11. Hoel Pond to Long Pond, St. Regis Canoe Area

Additional information: Paul Jamieson, *Adirondack Canoe Waters North Flow* and DEC brochure. The St. Regis Canoe Area is a wilderness filled with ponds and lakes. The area is southwest of Paul Smiths and north of Fish Creek Campground. The Hoel Pond to Long Pond canoe trip is just a sample of the circuits and two-car shuttles that can be made in this canoe area or in the Wild Forest to the south. Both regions are noted for their numerous ponds, evergreen-clad shores, good carry trails, and remote campsites.

When you leave a car at the take-out, walk down to Long Pond and check the wind. Northwest winds can make this a difficult paddle. You may want to reverse the direction of the trip or wait for a calmer day if winds are too strong.

Paddle from the Hoel Pond put-in 1.6 miles across that pond to Turtle Pond, then 0.9 miles northwest through Turtle to the narrow channel, then 0.6 mile across to the carry at the southern lobe of Slang Pond. Long Pond has many lobes to explore; the carry to the take-out is 2.4 miles away in the southwestern arm of the pond.

Distance - 5.9 miles plus 0.4 in two carries.
Time - A full day with exploring, two days with camping.
Put-in - Floodwood Road west of NY 30, first right on Hoel Pond Road, then left near golf course on narrow dirt road for 0.3 mile to put-in.
Take-out - DEC parking area on Floodwood Road, 5.25 miles from NY 30. There is a 0.2-mile carry from the parking area to Long Pond.
Shuttle - Floodwood Road.

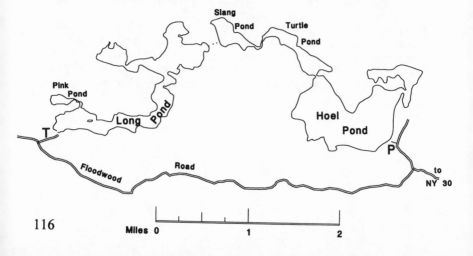

More Adventures

New York State has acquired new land for the Forest Preserve that allow canoers to enjoy two new waterways, Little Tupper Lake and the main branch of the Moose River. Funds for these acquisitions came from one of the Environmental Bond Acts. Both offer wonderful opportunities for canoeing. This section also contains two trips that were omitted from the first edition. The Saranac River is a two-car shuttle; the other is a wonderful chain of lakes.

The 1998 revision also adds two trips, pages 39 and 62, to replace outings on Piseco Outlet. The launch site on Piseco Outlet was acquired by private owners who have posted the put-in on NY 10. Would that the state could have acquired an easement here so we all could continue to canoe to Spy Lake or Big Bay.

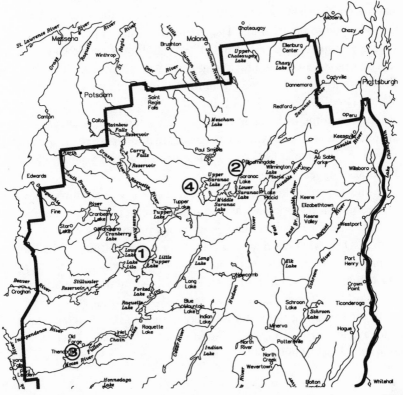

1. Whitney Park and Little Tupper Lake

We lost count of the loons after we tallied twenty-four. It was impossible to keep track of the mergansers and other ducks. Little Tupper Lake's scenic shoreline, bordered with a few huge pines and spruces, sandy beaches, and rock outcrops unfolds like a nature film. On a calm day, there are two versions of the film: the mirrored waters reveal an upside-down world that shimmers in the riffles of your canoe.

Little Tupper Lake was the largest privately held lake in the Adirondack Park. Now that the state has acquired it and the 15,000-acre tract surrounding, the lake is one of the most beautiful places in the Adirondacks to canoe. There is only one drawback: be sure to pick a calm day. The lake is over 5.5 miles long and winds and waves can be a problem. This is also an ideal area for canoe camping; an overnight at one of the newly designated campsites would let you explore another lake and streams or walk some of the logging roads that take you to other ponds. The state only acquired part of the Whitney property; the rest of it and two inholdings on the lake remain private. In the future, a long carry will be marked that will allow you to take your canoe from the Whitney property into Shingle Shanty Brook and on to Lake Lila.

Parking at the launch site is limited to 40 cars. Signs direct you to the put-in and tell you where you can camp and where roads are open to hiking. The ranger assigned to the area can answer your questions and make suggestions for your trip.

Little Tupper Lake makes a lazy curve from west southwest to east northeast. It is a broad lake, in places over a mile wide, but its sinuous shoreline reveals many bays, rocky promontories, and tiny islands. On a windless day, you can easily make a circuit of the lake. At present you can only canoe one other body of water on the tract-- Rock Pond. To reach it, find Rock Pond Outlet on the far southern shore of Little Tupper Lake. This stream twists and turns heading south for 1.5 miles, flat water interrupted by one short stretch where you have to carry your canoe. The carry is well-marked. Each side of triangular Rock Pond is over a mile long. There is a large, rock-rimmed island in the middle and several small rock islets near the south shore. Strong paddlers can reach Rock Pond and return in a day's outing, especially if conditions are right. Do not go so fast, though, that you miss the wildlife and the scenery.

Distance: 15 miles or more
Time: A full day or more if you camp out
Launch site: Both ends of county road 10 A (Sabattis Circle Road) intersect NY 30 between Long and Tupper lakes. They join to continue west as the Sabattis Road at a causeway at the outlet of Little Tupper Lake, about 3 miles from NY 30. Continue a little over a mile on Sabattis Road past the causeway to a marked parking area which abuts the former Whitney headquarters.

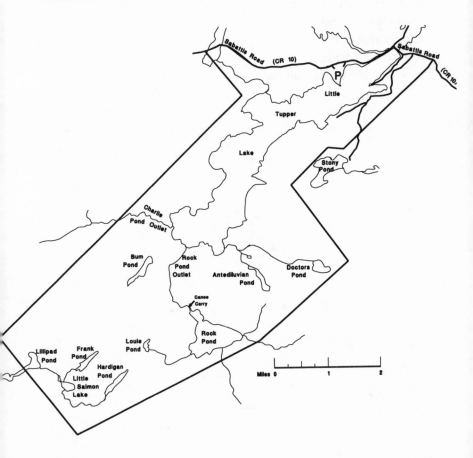

2. Saranac River

This two-car canoe trip is an adventure in contrasts. For much of the way you the river is not far from a major highway with trucks roaring by. But, the shores of the river have as rich a variety of shrubs and water plants and birds as you can find anywhere. We called it a twenty-one-heron trip because we saw that many great blue herons. Every stretch of river had a heron patrolling the shallows. Kingfishers sped past, alerting us to their presence with a rattle-like cry. Marshes along the river flash red with cardinal flower blooms in mid-summer.

The river is flat, but for most of the summer there is a strong enough current to sweep you along, making it very easy to paddle and making the trip seem shorter than it is. There are a few long straight stretch and many loops and ox-bows along the sinuous stretches.

The first 1.5 miles is the straightest and noisiest, but the high banks covered with flowering viburnums and other shrubs in spring, berries in late summer and fall are the prettiest of all the trip. At 1.5 miles the river passes a sewage treatment plant and passes under its access road. More straight stretches follow, but these are far from the road and bordered with great stretches of marsh. Moose Creek widens into a broad channel just before it joins the river from the east. Beyond tall forest borders the river, but most of the shoreline shows evidence of spring flooding. A long straight stretch ends in a series of squiggles and more marshy shores. Within sight of houses in Bloomingdale you pass the confluence with Sumner Brook at just over 7 miles. A short way beyond, the stream makes a sharp hairpin turn and changes course to easterly for the last 1.6 miles to the take-out by the bridge. The last section is the twisted with a dense border of alder marshes.

Distance: 9 miles

Time: 4 hours, but allow more for picnicking and nature watching

Put-in: There is a small park with a parking area at the intersection of Bloomingdale Avenue, NY 3, and Pine Street at the northern edge of Saranac Village. The put-in is just downstream from the bridge and below the short rapids.

Take-out: On the west side of Moose Pond Road just north of the bridge over the Saranac River.

Shuttle: To find the take-out from the put-in, drive north on NY 3 to Bloomingdale, and turn right in the hamlet, still following NY 3. Within 0.2 mile you cross the bridge over Sumner Brook. Take the right turn immediately past the bridge onto River Road. Follow it for just over 1.5 miles to a marked right turn onto Moose Pond Road. From here it is 0.4 mile to the take-out and the bridge over the Saranac River..

3. The Main Branch of the Moose River

A really novel adventure with a train ride for the shuttle

This is the most unusual canoe trip in the Adirondacks, but you have to make arrangements for it before you start. You will need a ticket for yourself and your canoe purchased at the Thendara Railroad Station. You can extend the trip by starting at Tichners in Old Forge (there is a fee and you can rent canoes here). Or, you can put your canoe in from the causeway over the river that is close enough to the rail station so that you can park at the station and walk to this put-in. Either way you will enjoy a superb downstream trip with lots of wildlife and beautiful vistas. And, you can have the thrill of putting your canoe on the old baggage car for the return shuttle.

Three cautions to observe: Allow plenty of time. Four hours is sufficient for a quick trip through, but not long enough to stop and enjoy the scenery. Water can be very low in dry summers, so there may be a few additional carries. And, the wind shooting down the west-facing straight stretches can make paddling strenuous.

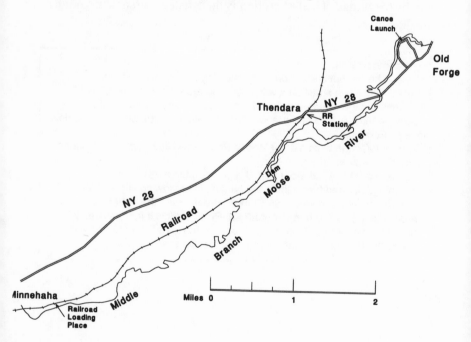

From Tichners paddle downstream for 0.75 mile to the confluence with the North Branch and turn south and under NY 28, continuing 1.25 miles more to the causeway. The last part is the same as the end of the trip described on page 106. Canoe under the causeway and head through the open water and around many patches of pickerel weed and shrubs that sometimes hide the main channel. You reach the dam 1.5 miles from the causeway; this section is described on page 64. In it you paddle through open areas with a view to the back of the railroad station.

When you reach the wooden dam, pull out on the left, south, side for the short carry around the dam. This grassy knoll here is a fine place for a picnic.

Beyond the river narrows and is overhung with tall trees making many pretty views. The river is shallow here and the current sometimes swift. Mileposts along the river tell you how long it will take to reach Minnehaha. With twists and turns, this section is over 4.5 miles long. When you see rapids ahead, look for a sign on your left for the beginning of the carry, which is about 150 yards long and quite narrow. When you put your canoe back in the river, you only have to paddle across to the far side to find the small dock that marks the take-out.

Distance:
Time: Six hours with the train ride, check the trail schedules and make reservations before you start.
Put-in: Tichners on River Road in Old Forge or the causeway across the Moose River. To find the alternate put-in, first locate the Thendara Railroad Station on NY 28, west of Old Forge. From the station, head east and make two right turns. The causeway is 0.5 mile from the station, a 10- to 15-minute walk.
Take-out: A small landing at Minnehaha. The railroad platform is up the steep bank to your right. The baggage car stops at this platform.
Shuttle: The railroad between Minnehaha and Thendara; a fee is charged, reservations required.

4. Four-Pond Circuit in the Saranac Wild Forest

The circuit of Follensby Clear, Polliwog, Little Polliwog, and Horseshoe ponds has many rewards: wonderful swimming, short carries, and undeveloped shoreline. From the launch site at the south end of Follensby Clear Pond, head out between two islands and through a narrow passage and around a peninsula. In the northern part of the pond there is a small island, whose far, northern, shore has great swimming.

From the island, head northwest to the carry to Polliwog Pond. The entrance sign may be obscured by bushes. The carry is short and steep. You can paddle into Polliwog's western bay and explore its quiet waters--a frequent osprey-nesting site. Or, turn south through the narrows and look for a sandy beach near a campsite set among towering pines. This is a good place to rest and swim.

Continue south across Polliwog to the carry on the southwestern shore. It leads to swampy Little Polliwog. A brief paddle and a short carry take you to Horseshoe Pond, a quiet secluded place where you should see loons. The prominent peninsula has more good swimming. The carry back to Follensby Clear is to the right of a large rock and campsite on the eastern shore, across from the peninsula. Head south through the narrows and back to the launch site.

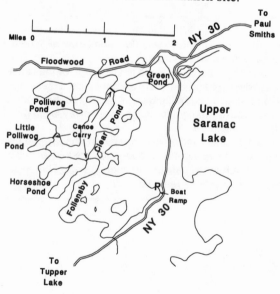

Distance - 6 miles or more
Time - Plan to spend all day.
Launch - There are two launch sites for Follensby Clear Pond. Choose the unmarked one, 0.7 miles north of the entrance to Fish Creek Campground on the northwest side of NY 30, just before the bridge over Spider Creek Passage. There is a small dock.

Other Brochures and Canoe Possibilities

Niagara Mohawk Power Corporation (NIMO) has 30 NIMO Recreation Areas, 24 of which have access for boaters. Nine have access for cartop boats and canoes only, so are more desirable for canoeing. A brochure describing these recreation areas is available at local NIMO offices upstate or write NIMO 300 Erie Blvd. West, Syracuse, NY 13202. NIMO has a separate brochure *Beaver River Canoe Route*.

Franklin County Department of Tourism, 63 West Main Street, Malone, NY 12953, 518-483-6767; *Canoe Routes in Southern Franklin County*.

Lewis County Office of Tourism, Lowville, NY, 13367. *Riverfest Brochure* describes the Black River in Lewis County.

Department of Environmental Conservation; In addition to the brochures noted in text. Note that not all the listed brochures are in print all of the time:

Saranac Islands; lake canoeing, island camping, reservations required.

New York State Boat Launching Sites, published jointly with Office of Parks and Recreation and Historic Preservation.

Fishing and Canoeing the Grass River, From DeGrasse to Massena, describes trip above Lampson Falls and routes outside the Adirondack Park.

Guide to Fishing the Indian River Lakes - The Indian has canoeable lakes northwest of the Adirondacks in Jefferson County.

The Raquette River in St. Lawrence County describes canoe routes from Piercefield Flow north through Carry Falls to Rainbow Falls reservoirs and on sections north outside the Adirondack Park to Massena.

Fishing and Canoeing the Oswegatchie River, Newton Falls to Ogdensburg, canoe routes described are in the northwestern Adirondacks and outside the Adirondack Park.

Adirondack Canoe Routes - Lake Chains, describes the Fulton Chain to the Saranac Lakes.

Stillwater Reservoir describes canoeing and designated camping areas.

Moose River Recreation Area describes access roads, designated camping areas, and lakes.

Bog River Flow describes canoeing and designated camping areas.

Index to Terms Used in the Text

Back strokes, 19
Beaver dams, 57
Blade, 13
Bog plants, 37
Boreal, 46
Bow, 11-12
Bow stroke, 14
Campgrounds, 32
Canoe types, 12
Car-top carrier, 25
Carrying a canoe, 24-25
Current, 20, 55
Draw stroke, 18
Easement, 43
Escarpment, 97
Esker, 45
Fault valley, 42
Feeder canal, 94-98
Forest Preserve, 42
Freeboard, 12
Getting in your canoe, 21
Getting out of your canoe, 22
Grip, 13
Gunwale, 12
Headwind, 31
J-stroke, 17
Keel, 11, 12

Kneeling, 23
Launching, 22
Maps, 8, 11
Meander, 59
Oxbow, 40
Paddle, 13
Portage, 25
Pry stroke, 18
Put-in, 24
Rapids, 11
Reverse sweep, 19
Riffles, 69
Shaft, 13
Shuttle, 24, 93
Snags, 47
Stern, 11-12
Strainers, 69
Sweep stroke, 16
Sweepers, 69
Take-out, 24
Throat, 13
Thwart, 12
Tipping over, 22
V, 69
Waves, 31
Wheeling cart, 25
Wind, 31

Index to Waterways

Alder Pond, 86-98
Auger Flats, 58
Ausable River, 67-68
Big Moose Lake, 77
Black Creek, 104
Black Pond, 48
Black River Canal, 96-98
Black River, 63
Blue Mountain Lake, 108-109
Bog River, 80
Bog River Falls, 62
Boquet River, 68
Brandreth Lake Outlet, 78
Brown's Tract Ponds Campground, 35
Buck Pond Campground, 36
Buck Pond, 65-66
Canada Lake, 59, 71
Cedar River Flow, 75-76
Chubb River, 87

Church Pond, 112-113
Deer River Flow, 49
Eagle Lake, 108-109
East Branch St. Regis River, 89
East Canada Creek, 59
Fall Lake, 72
Fall Stream, 72
Fish Creek Campground, 35
Follensby Clear Pond, 124
Forked Lake Campground, 34
Forked Lake, 78
Francis Lake, 45
Franklin Falls Pond, 50
Fulton Chain of Lakes, 107
G Lake, 53
Garnet Lake, 39
Good Luck Lake, 61
Grass River, 82-83, 110-111
Harrisburg Lake, 38

Hatch Brook, 114-115
Hitchins Pond, 80
Hoel Pond, 116
Horseshoe Lake, 46
Horseshoe Pond, 124
Hudson River Feeder Canal, 94-95
Hudson River, 100
Indian Lake (Moose River Plains), 44
Indian Lake, 41
Jabe Pond, 52
Jones Pond, 112-113
Kayuta Lake, 63
Kunjamuk River, 53, 74
Kushaqua Lake, 90
Kushaqua Narrows, 65-66
Lake Abanakee, 41
Lake Champlain, 91
Lake Durant Campground, 34
Lake Eaton Campground, 34
Lake Harris Campground, 34
Lake Lila, 79
Lampson Falls, 110-111
Lens Lake, 37
Lewey Lake Campground, 34
Lewey Lake, 62
Lily Lake, 59, 71
Limekiln Lake Campground, 35
Lincoln Pond Campground, 33
Little River, 81
Little Tupper Lake, 118
Long Pond, 116
Lost Ponds, 44
Lows Lake, 80
Luzerne Campground, 32
Main Branch Sacandaga River, 58, 74
Marion River, 108
Mason Lake, 41
Massawepie Mire, 82-83
McColloms Pond, 89
Meacham Lake Campground, 35
Meacham Lake, 89
Miami River, 62
Middle Branch Grass River, 110
Middle Branch Moose, 64
Mill Creek, 98
Moose Pond, 48
Moose River, 122-123
Moose River Plains, 76
Moss Lake, 44

Mud Lake, 62
Mud Pond, 73
Nelson Lake, 64
Newcomb Lake, 54
Nicks Lake Campground, 35
North Branch Moose River, 106-107
North Branch Saranac River, 65-66
North Lake, 43
Osgood Pond, 112-113
Osgood River, 35, 89, 112
Oxbow Lake, 40
Paradox Lake Campground, 33
Piercefield Flow, 47
Pine Lake, 39
Polliwog Pond, 124
Putnam Pond Campground, 32
Rainbow Lake, 90
Rainbow Narrows, 65-66
Raquette Lake, 65, 108
Raquette River, 47, 84-86
Rollins Pond Campground, 35
Sacandaga Lake, 73
Salmon River, 114-115
Saranac River, 50-51, 120-121
Schroon River, 66
Shingle Shanty Brook, 79
Simon Pond, 84
Slang Pond, 116
South Bay, 91
South Inlet, 65
South Pond, 42
Sprite Creek, 71
Stewarts Dam, 71
Stony Creek, 38, 101
Streeter Lake, 46
Thirteenth Lake, 42
Trout Brook, 66
Trout Lakes, 61, 102
Tupper Lake, 47
Turtle Pond, 116
Union Falls Pond, 50-51
Upper Kunjamuk, 53
Utowana Lake, 108-109
Vly Lake, 72
West Branch Sacandaga River,
    60-61, 102-103
West Lake, 59, 71
Whitney Park, 118-119

Barbara McMartin has written extensively about the Adirondacks. She has devoted herself to Adirondack causes and served as chairman of the Committee for the Adirondack Park Centennial. Her other books:

From *Lake View Press*
  To the Lake of the Skies

Discover the Adirondack Series, written with various co-authors
  Discover the Adirondack High Peaks
  Discover the Central Adirondacks
  Discover the Eastern Adirondacks
  Discover the Northeastern Adirondacks
  Discover the Northwestern Adirondacks
  Discover the Northern Adirondacks
  Discover the South Central Adirondacks
  Discover the Southeastern Adirondacks
  Discover the Southern Adirondacks
  Discover the Southwestern Adirondacks
  Discover the West Central Adirondacks

Books from Countryman Press
  Fifty Hikes in the Adirondacks, Second Edition

From NORTH COUNTRY BOOKS
  Hides, Hemlocks and Adirondack History
  The Great Forest of the Adirondacks
  Adventures in Hiking
    A Young Peoples' Guide to the Adirondacks
  Fun on Flatwater
    An Introduction to Adirondack Canoeing
  Adventures in Camping
    An Introduction to Adirondack Backpacking

McMartin's Books are distributed by
NORTH COUNTRY BOOKS

W. Alec Reid, Barbara's husband, has retired from IBM and has produced maps and charts for Barbara's most recent works.

Gregory Palestri was trained in architecture and art at The Cooper Union in New York City and has done illustrations for *Adirondack Life*.